Praise for *New Tricks*

"At Resurrection, we've seen how pet ministry builds connection, healing, and community. *New Tricks* offers inspiring stories and practical steps for churches ready to embrace all of God's creatures. It's a heartfelt call to a ministry of compassion and care."
—**Adam Hamilton**, Senior Pastor, Church of the Resurrection, and author of *Wrestling with Doubt, Finding Faith*

"In a time when it is vitally important for churches to find ways to make meaningful connections in an increasingly difficult world, Snyder and Fiser have offered us wonderful 'new tricks' for tending to the sacred relationship between animals and humans—a sentiment that knows no religious boundaries. You will find so many ideas to spark delight and increase compassion and participation inside and beyond your community. Every church can benefit from this study filled with inspiring stories and helpful resources!"
—**Dr. Marcia McFee**, creator of Worship Design Studio and author of *Purveyors of Awe: Curating a Life of Spiritual Depth*

"This book is built on what our experience, even our DNA, tells us—that animal companions help make us more human. I appreciate how the authors start with unconditional love and loyalty but then move on to reveal how animal friends lead the way in creating community, building respect, encouraging play and teamwork, and looking out for those in need. This is a book we need."
—**Jon M. Sweeney**, author of *Sit in the Sun: And Other Lessons in the Spiritual Wisdom of Cats*

"This book so deftly defines and describes the importance and benefits of the 'human-companion animal bond' without explicitly using the term. The book recounts how the souls of both animals and their caretakers are nurtured by this bond. The authors thoughtfully remind us how the unconditional love that pets provide their humans can be a metaphor for God's unconditional love for us. With its thought-provoking questions, I recommend this book for use by animal lovers as a small group book study as well as a guide for instituting a pet ministry in their own church."
—**Jon Kendall**, DVM

NEW TRICKS

HOW **PET MINISTRY** CAN TRANSFORM FAITH COMMUNITIES AND CHANGE LIVES

BETSY SINGLETON SNYDER AND GAYLE MCKUIN FISER

NEW TRICKS: How Pet Ministry Can Transform Faith Communities and Change Lives

At the time of publication all websites referenced in this book were valid. However, due to the fluid nature of the internet, some addresses may have changed or the content may no longer be relevant.

ISBN: 978-0-8358-2074-5

Epub ISBN: 978-0-8358-2075-2

Cover design: Cary Smith

Interior design: PerfecType, Nashville, TN

For more information on resources available from The Upper Room

call 1-800-972-0433 or visit www.upperroom.org

From Betsy

In memory of Bishop Kenneth W. Hicks, the first Christian leader I knew who loved dogs as family, who assured me they would be in heaven because heaven would not be heaven without dogs, who sat with me when I had to say goodbye to a beloved dog, and whose name was given to Bishop, my loving, gracious golden retriever, the dog who saved my life.

From Gayle

To Paul, Penny, and Yvonne and all the dogs who taught us that love is wide, love is deep, and love never dies.

TABLE OF CONTENTS

PART THREE:
A Field Guide for Creating Pet Ministries

INTRODUCTION
A Tale of Two Pet People

From Betsy

I remember exactly when I became emotionally attached to a dog for the first time. My parents' twenty-seven-year marriage had always been rocky as a result of my father's alcoholism, fueled by his undiagnosed bipolar condition. Nevertheless, somehow, in the midst of his addiction, my folks had raised my three older brothers and a sister. Now grown, all of my siblings were either in college, in the Air Force, or married.

It was then that my mother decided she was absolutely done riding this emotional roller coaster, regardless of her financial concerns. She would take me, her youngest child and just six years old at the time, and start over. We would get out of the chaos. She would work her modest, secure government job and pay off the leftover debt from my father's poor choices. While her decision was certainly the best one she could make, we were also left vulnerable whenever the rent was raised, which occurred regularly. Our newly single-income home left her without the means to hire a babysitter, so I became a latchkey kid. Eventually, mom allowed me to get a dog as a companion. Back then, dogs slept in doghouses outside, and Frisky, our adopted mutt, did too. But that was fine by me because I was already outside much of the time.

When my mother remarried, I was entering sixth grade and just hitting puberty. Anxiety, which I did not yet have a name for, accompanied all the dramatic changes in my world. I don't think I could have described my emotions at that time to any human. I don't even think I knew what they were.

Years before the marriage, my stepdad had built our new home. A country boy and handy guy, he had also built a dog pen toward the back of our nearly one-acre lot. Two doghouses, each filled with hay, sat side by side. My stepfather had a handsome bird dog, a setter named Freckles, who had white fur with brown spots and a seemingly permanent smile. He was a new friend for Frisky. Because we now lived off of a highway rather than in a neighborhood where I could play with other kids, I spent most evenings in the backyard dog pen, taking food and water to our two dogs and visiting with them. Once my caretaking chores were done, I'd climb on top of the largest doghouse and talk to Frisky and Freckles for long stretches of time. I told them about all the changes in my life, what I liked and what made me sad and unhappy. And as those dogs listened, the anxiety inside of me eased—at least for a little while.

My love of dogs was also shaped by the books I read as a child. Quite a few were about people and their dogs—*Sounder*, *Old Yeller*, *Where the Red Fern Grows*, and *The Call of the Wild*. In each of these stories, some human, often a child, had their life transformed by a dog. That's when I think I knew, somewhere deep inside of myself, that I would always have a dog. And my dog would live inside of my house!

I have a newer, but well-worn book called *Good Dog* that contains a collection of dog stories by popular writers. The stories first appeared in a column in the Southern lifestyle magazine *Garden and Gun*. Each story reminded me of how dogs can shape our lives. Even the dogs that challenge us, like the one described in the popular book *Marley and Me*, can push us to love more deeply. Sometimes it's the difficult, inconvenient personalities—whether in animals or people—that teach us to love better.

In the early 2000s, I was serving as a pastor at an urban church known for drawing in unconventional seekers. Many of them were willing to take risks and try new ministries to reach out and serve the community. During one of our leadership team meetings, we were brainstorming about how to engage with our neighborhood in ways that most churches wouldn't consider. I mentioned that I liked the idea of some kind of therapy dog ministry. After all, we already held an animal blessing every year. We even had a chihuahua as a regular attendee in worship. Her name was Chloe, and she sat serenely in her human momma's lap, decked out in her best pearls and occasionally a pink frock.

I had barely finished mentioning the therapy dog idea when one of our leaders, Gayle, said that she believed she could create a therapy dog team. She could make that happen.

From Gayle

Penny was my first dog, and you never forget your first. I was probably five years old when Penny came to live with our family. She was a small, smooth-coated rat terrier mix with a white body and brown on both her head and the tip of her tail. Penny needed a home, and three young children growing up on twenty acres needed a dog.

Since I was the only girl among my brothers, Penny became my ally. She happily joined me for tea parties and would let me dress her up in clothes for a stroll in my doll's carriage. Living with Penny throughout my childhood would forever shape my relationship with pets—they became family. That first special bond planted the seed for what would become a lifelong love of dogs.

In mid-life, my husband, Paul, and I were searching for a new puppy after one of our favorite dogs had died. We were established in our careers, but our house had become too quiet. We missed the click-click-clicking sound of paws on our hardwood floors.

Our hearts ached for the loss of our fourteen-year-old girl, a dog we had raised from a litter we had helped deliver. We'd held her in our arms since she was just two days old. Over the years, our dogs had become our children.

For me, our unexpected journey into pet ministry began on a bright spring day with one particular puppy. That morning, I had read a devotional titled "Wonders Will Unfold." My husband and I were still apprehensive, uncertain about our expectations, as we arrived to meet who might be our newest family member.

We spent time watching and playing with all the puppies, observing how they interacted with each other. One pup was very striking, such a beauty. We chose her, but then we noticed another puppy, isolated from the others, seemingly worn out from too much roughhousing with her playmates. She seemed to be taking a needed rest.

Our sweet dog who had recently died had a unique habit: she would gently nibble Paul's ear. She would also curl her body up around his neck. Imagine our surprise when Paul picked up the resting puppy and she did exactly that—nibbled his ear and snuggled around his neck in that same familiar, loving way. In that indescribable moment, we felt an overwhelming connection with this puppy. It was as if we were receiving a divine nudge, a voice whispering, "Yes. Pick this one!"

This second puppy wasn't conventionally perfect. Her facial markings were asymmetrical, she had an eyelash growing from the side of her right eye, and one of her legs was slightly injured. But to us, she was perfect. That day, we didn't go home with only the one puppy we'd planned to adopt but a second one as well. And that marked the beginning of a brand-new adventure in our lives.

When our girls were a year old, Paul bumped into a former teaching colleague he hadn't seen in many years. She had retired and become a professional dog trainer. She said, "If you ever want to get your dogs certified as therapy dogs, I can teach a class for you."

The very next week, I was in a meeting at our church. We were sharing about our dogs when our pastor, Betsy, said, "Oh, that reminds me. I've been thinking we need to get our dogs trained as therapy dogs to visit people around here." I raised my hand and said, "I can make that happen!" And just like that, our pet ministry began—sparked by a layperson with a passion for dogs and a pastor who loved animals and shared the vision.

Our Observations about Pets in a Changing Cultural Landscape

Up until that moment, our church's primary connection to pets had been through our annual animal blessing—a joyful event that celebrates the presence of pets in people's lives. But as time passed, we began to realize that this gathering was about more than just honoring the gift of beloved animals and their bond with their caregivers. There was a larger cultural shift happening. American attitudes were changing. People were investing more time, space, and resources into their pets.

Retailers caught on quickly and were actively targeting pet families. These people weren't just buying pet food; they were curating entire lifestyles around their animal companions. Orvis, long known for its hunting and fly-fishing gear, began featuring high-end dog products, like attractive beds pictured with winsome pups lounging comfortably. L.L.Bean released house shoes featuring cats and dogs. A booming niche of ultra-customized pet products emerged: personalized pajamas with your pet's face on them, or stately portraits reimagining your cat as period royalty or a dignified colonel.

As we paid more attention to people and their pets in different congregational settings, we found others who were willing to exchange ideas and collaborate about what a ministry with animals might look like. Resurrection United Methodist Church in Kansas, a much larger congregation with an established pet ministry, enthusiastically shared ideas, ranging from continuing education about pets to pastoral care to outreach activities in the community.

Inspired, we began to send pet parents a handwritten note acknowledging when they got a new pet or when there was a pet loss in the family. We partnered with a sewing ministry at our church to create special pet prayer blankets that we gave to pet parents to mark special milestones. These fleece blankets, lovingly sewn and stitched with an embroidered cross, were prayed over, tied with a bow, and presented to a church member—or to their friends and family—as the need arose. Later, we designed custom grief cards for pet loss that would accompany the blankets.

Word spread. As we saw emotional social media posts from grieving pet parents sharing memories and photos, it became even clearer: most people consider their pets family. We began delivering more and more blankets. Many recipients were moved to tears, and the gesture brought comfort amid their loss.

From those early days in 2007, our pet ministry grew. We expanded and began supporting local rescue efforts, donating pet food to food pantries, offering educational resources about pet care, partnering with local veterinarians, raising funds for emergency treatments, and even helping families find and adopt pets suited to both their lifestyle and the animal's long-term needs. We noticed two trends converging—more people embracing pets as family, and fewer people participating in traditional faith communities. If churches already offer ministries for other family members, we thought, why not for their animal companions as well?

The first section of this book, "For the Love of Animals," examines how our relationships with pets can help us become better people—more attuned to our connections with both animals and one another. We explore some of the traditional spiritual practices and attitudes that can be nurtured through regular connection with animals.

The second section, "For the Love of Neighbors," considers how pets can teach us to be better neighbors, especially when it comes to loving people who are different from us. It's a reminder that respect, hospitality, and the ability to create inclusive and healthy communities are all practices we can learn through our bonds with animals.

In the final section, "A Field Guide for Creating Pet Ministry," we offer examples of pet ministries and community service initiatives across a wide array of areas. Our goal is to help more people experience the deep, transformative connection between humans and animals and recognize the interconnectedness of all living things.

We especially want to speak to and encourage people who no longer feel connected to a faith community—or who never have. Instead of focusing on "correct" beliefs, we encourage a shift toward love, kinship, and a shared commitment to the well-being of all creation. For us, love is the heart of the Christian tradition. Divine love does not separate or segregate us—it unites. We believe that our animals can draw us closer to God and to each other, and we invite you to discover the same joy.

Discussion Questions

1. Reflect on your own personal experiences with your pets. How have pets changed your perception about the human-animal connection?
2. Have you noticed an increasing prominence in the presence of pets in public spaces and in media? If so, how has it changed your awareness of the ways pets fit into family life?
3. Have you ever participated in an activity to support or help animals in your faith community or with neighbors? What did you learn about yourself?

2. [illegible]

PART ONE

For the Love of Animals

"Surely we ought to show kindness and gentleness to animals for many reasons and chiefly because they are of the same origin as ourselves."
—Saint John Chrysostom[1]

"Without close and reciprocal relationships with other animal beings, we're alienated from the rich, diverse, and magnificent world in which we live."
—Marc Bekoff[2]

1. Saint John Chrysostom, quoted in *Compassion for Animals*, ed. Andrew Linzey and Tom Regan (London: SPCK, 1988), 65.
2. Marc Bekoff, *The Emotional Lives of Animals: A Leading Scientist Explores Animal Joy, Sorrow, and Empathy—and Why They Matter* (Novato, CA: New World Library, 2008), 24.

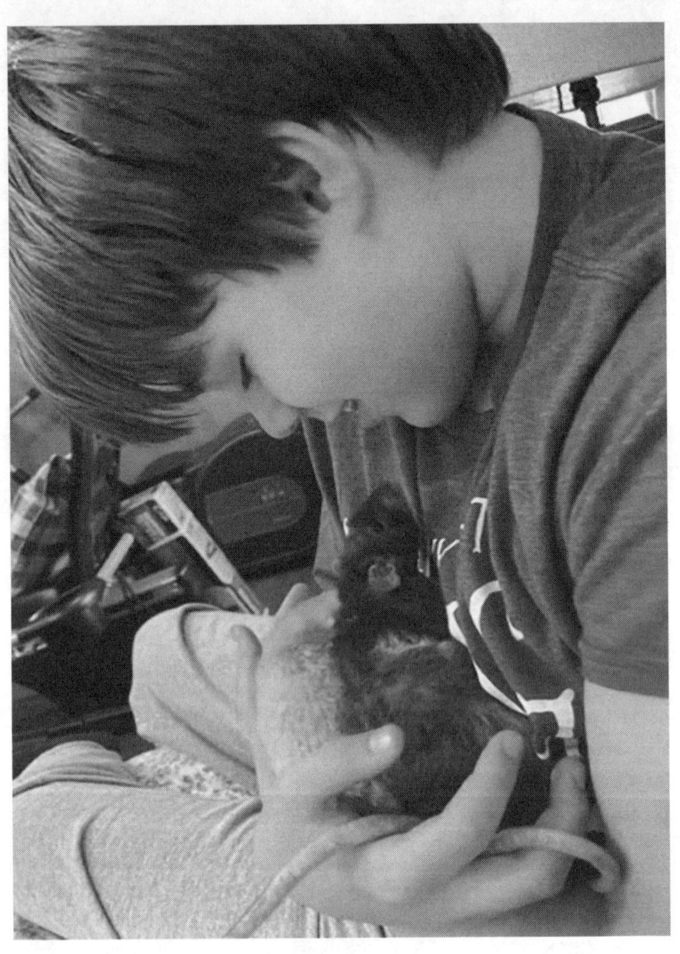

CHAPTER 1

Why We Care for All Creatures

Many who practice the Christian faith tradition believe that animals—humans included—share in God's broad covenant. Likewise, plenty of other folks across the religious spectrum, even those who identify as spiritual-but-not-religious or something similar, also recognize the sacredness of animals as part of an interconnected creation. Our Christian tradition, along with several others, teaches that God has invited humans to produce good things for the earth and all its creatures.

But what does that mean?

In the book of Genesis, the narrator offers a beautiful, poetic account of the creation story, how the world came into being. According to this story, God made the animals on the fifth and sixth days of creation. The animals, like humans, received a shared blessing to "be fruitful and multiply" (Gen. 1:22), affirming their inherent value to God. All living beings are meant to contribute; all are meant to replenish the earth.

This version of the creation story states that humans, made in God's image, have a special role in creation—one of "dominion" (Gen. 1:26). While some have interpreted "dominion" as a license for exploitation, the larger Christian tradition teaches that it carries a responsibility to care for creation. As part of this world, humans are not only responsible for creation but also accountable to the other animals and to the earth itself.

Our vocation is to nurture and protect creation, contributing to its flourishing, not for the long-held idea of the creation's utility but for its own intrinsic, sacred worth. Our call is to create something good, just like our Creator. We can choose to work alongside creation as partners, fostering life and goodness, or we can harm it, diminishing its vitality and ironically harming ourselves in the process. Ultimately, we can either cooperate with God's intention for creation or undermine its interdependence and fruitfulness.

In *Laudato Si'*: *On Care for Our Common Home*, Pope Francis addressed a wide array of issues related to our shared environment and climate change. He emphasized that "the Church does not simply state that other creatures are completely subordinated to the good of human beings, as if they have no worth in themselves and can be treated as we wish."[1] Think about it like this: when we enjoy the companionship of domestic animals and benefit from their presence in our lives, we owe them abundant lives in return. They depend on us. This dependence means we have a responsibility to provide them with fulfilling lives.

That's why we share the belief that communities of faith "could take the lead in helping 'owners' to understand that we do not, properly speaking, 'own' animals at all; they are first and foremost creatures of God."[2] Recognizing this connection can deepen our sense of responsibility and compassion, encouraging a more conscious, respectful, and loving relationship with all living things in creation, and may remind humans that we have too often hindered and harmed life for the sake of our own consumption.

In our United Methodist tradition, John Wesley, the founder of the Methodist movement believed, "Human beings must live into their

1. Francis, *Laudato Si': On Care for Our Common Home* (Vatican City: Libreria Editrice Vaticana, 2015), §69.
2. Andrew Linzey, *Animal Rites: Liturgies of Animal Care* (Eugene, OR: Wipf and Stock, 1999), 57–58.

status and role as the image of God for the benefit of the nonhuman creation. Original humans, [as depicted in the creation story], had the ability to see 'with unspeakable pleasure, the order, the beauty, the harmony, of all creatures.' "[3] Thus, creation should be a space where humans, nonhumans, and God meet and exist together—ideally a sacred and holistic relationship.

Consider Francis of Assisi, the well-known 11th-century saint—the same friar from whom Pope Francis took his papal name—who called his fellow animals "brother" and "sister." Using these names for other creatures helps us recognize our shared origin in God and our responsibility for creation God has entrusted to us. In some sense, St. Francis offered Christians a way to see themselves as part of the creation and not separate from it, and to redefine family to include the natural world of which we are a part.

Similarly, Steven Charleston of the Choctaw Nation, who is also a retired Episcopal bishop, explains, "In order to receive the exchange offered by Native American tradition, we must put down the idea that the earth is nothing more than a vast accumulation of natural resources. Instead, we must see the earth as a living presence. We must recognize the interrelatedness of all life and begin to actively engage in protecting and learning from all our relations."[4] Like St. Francis, Charleston makes it clear that we and the rest of creation are all in this together.

While our faith background originates within the Methodist tradition, most of the world's major religions and wisdom traditions teach respect and care for animals, including the active prohibition of cruelty or mistreatment. Judaism, via the Talmud, teaches a slight variation of the Golden Rule: that which is hateful to you, do not do to your fellow. Islam generally upholds the belief that animals are aware of God, while Hindus and Sikhs believe all living creatures have souls. Jainism,

3. Andrew Linzey, *Animal Theologians* (New York: Oxford University Press, 2023), 79–80.

4. Steven Charleston, *Ladder to the Light: An Indigenous Elder's Meditations on Hope and Courage* (Minneapolis: Broadleaf Books, 2021), 140–41.

an ancient Indian religion, emphasizes non-violence and the welfare of all creatures. Buddhism promotes ecological mindfulness and generally supports the interdependence of all life. Native American tribal traditions remind us that our survival depends on the earth, and we must help it thrive in return.

Even many who hold no religious beliefs recognize the interconnected nature of creation and are actively involved in caring for and loving animals. What unites us is the shared awareness that animals, particularly domestic animals, rely on our compassion, care, and protection.

Discussion Questions

1. How has your faith or spiritual perspective informed your ideas about God, humanity, animals, and creation?
2. In what ways has viewing the natural world as a gift influenced how you live and interact with creation, particularly with animals?
3. Many religious traditions emphasize respect and care for animals. How does your faith impact your relationship with animals and the way you treat them?
4. In what ways do you think faith communities can work together to promote compassion and care for animals and the environment?

CHAPTER 2

Pets Are Friends and Family Who Make Us Better People

Stacy loves dogs! She's just crazy about them. She has spent years working in rescue and advocating for stronger laws to protect domestic animals. In her retirement, she decided to scale back on some of her more time-consuming efforts and chose to focus on adopting the most elderly dogs she could find from local rescue organizations. She lovingly refers to these older dogs as her "hospice dogs" and commits herself to making their last days as full of love and joy as possible. Stacy's kindness, unconditional love, devotion, and presence shine through in her commitment to giving these animals the care and dignity they deserve at the end of life.

The actions we take reflect who we are. They also shape who we become. When we practice kindness and compassion in one circumstance, we learn to be more kind and more compassionate in others. This behavior becomes a virtuous cycle in which we grow in love as we show love to others.

We truly believe that the animals we live with—our dogs, cats, turtles, and birds—have the ability to make us better humans.

Of course, this isn't only true with regard to animals, it's true for all of creation. Many faith communities, nonprofits, civic groups, and community development organizations share a common commitment to make the world a better place by serving those in need, including our animals and all of the planet. Eco-conscious groups also dedicate themselves to caring for creation—protecting the planet through recycling initiatives, green energy advocacy, land conservation efforts, and environmental stewardship. Since the earth cannot speak for itself, we can serve as a voice for the natural world, for all life.

The connectedness of the planet, where plants, insects, animals, and humans live together, is increasingly affected by natural disasters. These events can wreak havoc on the lives of people and their pets, resulting in the need for care and interventions that heal.

When Gayle volunteered at a pop-up resource event for survivors of thirteen deadly tornadoes in our state of Arkansas, she met many pet parents in need of support. The devastation left both humans and animals displaced and destabilized. One couple, whose home had been severely damaged, received a voucher to stay in a hotel with their two dogs. Determined to provide structure, routine, and safety for their pets, they adjusted their work schedules so that their dogs would never be left alone. Their commitment to their animal companions shaped their daily lives, ensuring that even in the midst of chaos, their pets remained safe and cared for.

Storms are only one type of destabilizing event during which people require support and care. When a mental health crisis occurs, pet parents may need assistance. One pet parent we know suffered through a severe episode of depression and anxiety, leading her to consider ending her life. She was also struggling with physical health issues that resulted in the loss of her job. With no stable housing, she found herself living out of her car with her dogs.

Recognizing that she needed help, she reached out to a friend who connected her with someone in our church community. That person, a dog lover with a large backyard, was willing to foster her two dogs. With her pets in safe hands, she was able to enter treatment while other friends and professionals stepped in to help her navigate the painful challenges that had led to this crisis in her life. Stories like hers are becoming more frequent, and we see more and more requests from medical facilities to assist with pet fostering when patients have long-term hospitalizations or physical therapy. These people worked together to offer spiritual and practical care.

The reality of basic requirements for life become sharply defined in a crisis. This is true both for people and for pets. An animal's basic needs become especially urgent when their caregiver is incapacitated. When a pet parent suddenly falls ill, loses their home, or suffers from a mental health crisis, their animals face perilous circumstances. These situations call us to step up, offer support, and ensure that both people and their beloved pets receive the care they need.

Animals Beyond Our Homes

Domestic animals in our homes are not the only creatures whose care can transform us. Animal rescue efforts extend far beyond household pets, encompassing a wide range of species that rely on organized care, dedicated volunteers, secure spaces, and community support.

One such organization, the Peaceful Valley Donkey Rescue (PVDR), operates in multiple states and works closely with various agencies to rescue abused, neglected, and abandoned donkeys. PVDR has conducted rescue operations in thirty-three states, partnering with the United States Fish and Wildlife Service, the Department of Agriculture, local sheriff's departments, and other refuge facilities. Rescuing larger domestic animals—many of whom are intelligent, affectionate, and have long lifespans like donkeys—requires coordinated effort. Ensuring the well-being of these animals depends on developing large safe spaces and fostering collaboration among organizations and individuals committed to their care.

Veterinarians support the care and health of all kinds of animals. After leading a church workshop on pet ministry, we met two attendees who are veterinarians—Drs. Jon and Jeanie Kendall. As professionals, they provide daily care for all kinds of pets as well as the people who love them.

Beyond their local work, they also offer both short-term and long-term support to underserved communities across the United States and around the world through an organization called Christian Veterinary Mission.

Through this group, Jon and Jeanie assist people whose animals need medical care but for whom such care is unavailable or too costly. For many, their animals are not just companions but also essential elements of their livelihood. These people care deeply for their animals and want them to be healthy and get the care they need. Jon and Jeanie's work helps overcome the financial and logistical challenges faced by these caregivers and ensure that both they and their animals are supported.

The bonds we make with our pets not only deepen our care and nurture for animals but also strengthen our connections with one another. These relationships can deepen our capacity for spiritual practices such as unconditional love, mindfulness, stability, purpose, loyalty, devotion, and greater awareness. Through our connection with pets, we gain a greater understanding of ourselves and others.

Discussion Questions

1. Think about a beloved childhood pet. In what ways did this pet help make you a better person?
2. When caring for an animal, what daily tasks or routines are meaningful to you? How can they become powerful rituals in your life?
3. How have your relationships with pets influenced the way you connect with and understand other people?
4. In what ways do you think caring for animals can strengthen qualities like compassion, patience, and mindfulness in our daily lives?

CHAPTER 3

Unconditional Love

Way too many of us struggle to feel deep love and acceptance from others. In American culture, we are often judged by material success, youth, beauty, intelligence, and social status. However, the reality of grace and unconditional love remind us that God's love is not about what we have, our connections, or how we measure up to external standards of perfection. Divine love is a gift offered without conditions or expectations. We are loved simply as we are.

Our animal friends embody this kind of love. They *do* see us as we are, and their love and affection do not falter—so long as we do not break their trust through mistreatment or neglect. While they do not judge us the way that humans can, they have their own perceptions of us and our behavior. Sometimes, their actions even mirror our own dysfunctions, offering us an unexpected reflection of ourselves and revealing areas where we need to grow and change.

Author E. B. Bartels writes, "When people learn to care about pets, they learn how to care for other beings outside of themselves, and that in turn can make them more empathetic, more generous, more kind to their fellow humans."[1] Fostering bonds between people and animals is important because we've seen firsthand the significant and positive impact of animals on human lives and how human love can help restore the health and wholeness of an animal.

Many of us have read the classic children's book *Charlotte's Web* by E. B. White. Charlotte, a clever barn spider, saves Wilbur the pig's life by weaving intelligent, flattering words into her webs—strategically placed above Wilbur to influence the way humans perceive him. Wilbur feels unworthy of her praise and asks his friend Charlotte, "Why did you do all this for me? . . . I don't deserve it. I've never done anything for you."

"'You have been my friend,' replied Charlotte. 'That in itself is a tremendous thing.'"[2]

We've witnessed how bonds between humans and animals can foster unconditional love and create a shared relationship. Consider the story of Anna and Anthony. They are dog people who have both fostered and adopted pets. Two days after finalizing the adoption of Ellie, their third and supposedly final four-legged family member, they received an unexpected call from the rescue organization, asking if they could foster another dog. Anna, assuming her husband would say no, responded that she needed to check with him first. She fully expected Anthony to say, "Absolutely not. We don't have room." However, to her astonishment, he said the opposite.

That very evening, they were on their way to pick up Arthur for the weekend. The initial plan was to keep him temporarily—just until he could see the vet and be placed in a more permanent home. Anna recalled scooping this sad little dog up into her lap, imagining how she would shower him with love.

He was only supposed to stay for a few days before moving on to his forever home, but Arthur was far sicker than they had realized. He

1. E. B. Bartels, *Good Grief: On Loving Pets, Here and Hereafter* (New York: Mariner Books, 2022), 38.
2. E. B. White, *Charlotte's Web* (New York: Harper & Brothers, 1952), 164.

was malnourished, flea-infested, and heartworm positive. In addition to these conditions, he had a grade-four heart murmur and spinal nerve damage from a previous dog attack. He could not see well and was terrified of anyone petting or touching him. If anyone got too close to his face, he would snap at them out of fear. Looking at him, Anna thought to herself, "This poor little dog. I don't see how the rescue would even want to invest in him."

But rescue him they did. Anna and Anthony invested in Arthur, as did their family, friends, and church community. Arthur experienced the best life they could offer as he endured the painful treatments for heartworm disease. Later, he received a blessing at the church's annual Blessing of the Animals service. Arthur even participated in two parades, riding in his very own stroller that Anthony proudly pushed, making sure Arthur felt like part of their "pack."

Over time, the couple earned Arthur's trust, and he slowly began to seek affection from people. He couldn't run, jump, or play like other dogs, but he offered so much more. Anna and Anthony came to believe that Arthur was meant to be part of their family—that in caring for him through his sickness and pain, they, too, were being healed. They all needed each other.

As Arthur's condition deteriorated, they realized their role had shifted. They were no longer just his rescuers; they were his family, providing hospice care and ensuring that Arthur's final days were filled with love, comfort, and the dignity he deserved.

Despite the difficulties caring for Arthur, they believe he taught them a great deal about compassion, humility, and the true meaning of care—especially when someone has difficulty in returning love due to past trauma.

Reflecting on this journey, the couple shared, "To love and care for those who can love and care for us in return is nice, but it is when we love someone or something that may never be able to return that affection that we are living out our Christianity."

Love without strings expects nothing in return. A legitimate and much-needed way for people of faith and others to practice unconditional love is to consider focusing a pet ministry on fostering and rescue. Both do not necessarily lead to long term relationships, but offer fertile ground for us to grow in our capacity to love others unreservedly, knowing that we are helping a creature of God on a difficult part of their life's journey.

Discussion Questions

1. From a Christian perspective, God's love is a gift—always available and not dependent on human actions or responses. How does this understanding of unconditional love remind you of relationships you've had with pets?
2. Have you ever felt deeper love and acceptance from a beloved pet than from a person? How did that love change you?
3. In what ways have your pets taught you about grace, forgiveness, or loyalty—especially during times when you felt undeserving of love and support?
4. How might the love we receive from animals inspire us to extend more compassion to others—especially those who, like Arthur, may struggle to trust or love in return?

CHAPTER 4

Mindfulness and Presence

When Betsy's boys were younger, they often shared observations about the behaviors of family pets, including creative phrases they picked up from cartoons or videos. When one of their cats, Cougar, took to sitting with his legs tucked completely underneath himself with his eyes half-closed, he seemed serene and relaxed. Wyatt remarked that Cougar was in the "roast chicken" pose. "What?" Betsy asked, a bit confused. "You know!" Wyatt said, "He looks like a roast chicken." From then on, every time Betsy noticed this cat in the "chicken pose," it was hard to resist the calm cat vibe.

Companion animals help humans live better by reducing stress, alleviating depression, addressing certain mental health challenges, and even expanding our ability to be present in the moment. A connection to the natural rhythms of the world allows us to step away from the demands of the clock. In New Testament Greek, there are multiple words that can be translated as "time." The first is *chronos*, which refers to measured, sequential time, like the time on a clock or a calendar. However, there is another word, *kairos*, that also translates as "time" but has much less to do with the hours in a day. Instead, this word is about the opportune time, the right time—God's time. This suggests that our self-imposed schedules and obsessions with deadlines do not reflect the fullest experience God intends for us. A helpful way to express this idea is to recognize the importance of shifting from "clock time" to "creation time."

The gift of presence is especially valuable in a culture driven by competition and a preoccupation with clock time. We are constantly bombarded with images—particularly through social media—that intend to distract us and consume our time and energy. We become absorbed in others' curated content which often represents an idealized version of reality rather than genuine life experience. The result can lead to mental and emotional exhaustion, as well as a tendency to dwell too much on the past or worry too much about the future—forgetting that life only truly exists in the present. Mindfulness is the practice of embracing each moment and each minute as it unfolds, accepting it without critique or judgment.

Thankfully, humans are inherently connected to the natural world. We are part of it, and it is a part of us. We often forget this connection, losing ourselves in a maze of diversions, worry, and anxiety. Pets can help us reconnect—to the present moment, to others, to life itself.

Franciscan author Richard Rohr writes that his black lab of fifteen years, Venus, was for him an incarnation of the Divine Presence—the Christ:

> Venus taught me how to be present to people and let them be present to me through the way she always sought out and fully enjoyed my company for its own sake. She was always so eager to be with me, even if I interrupted her in the middle of the night to go with me on a sick call. She literally modeled for me how to be present to God and how God must be present to me . . . Presence is always reciprocal, or it is not presence at all.[1]

1. Richard Rohr, *The Universal Christ: How a Forgotten Reality Can Change Everything We See, Hope For, and Believe* (New York: Convergent Books, 2019), 132.

The Ministry of Presence with Animals

A Wesley Foundation college ministry in our area that serves two campuses invited our therapy dogs and their handlers to be on-site for holiday events around Halloween and Valentine's Day. The pups greeted students, faculty, and even the president of one of the colleges. This visit provided an opportunity for the campus community to de-stress, take a break from their hectic schedules and academic demands, and simply enjoy a moment of presence and playfulness. Two of the dogs sported costumes, a hotdog and a devil, which brought smiles and laughter from students.

Medical professionals are immersed in caring for others, which can deplete their emotional resilience. Gayle and her husband, Paul, responded to a request from CARTI (Central Arkansas Radiation Therapy Institute), a nonprofit treating cancer patients, to bring therapy dogs for Nurses Appreciation Week. The presence of therapy dogs helped these dedicated medical professionals momentarily step away from their demanding work and savor the simple joy of petting a sweet dog. It was not uncommon to see the nurses kneeling on the floor, giving the dogs belly rubs, fully immersed in the moment. Other handlers and their dogs have also visited medical staff, including a retreat for ER nurses, who handle work in high-pressure environments where they are required to make rapid, life-saving decisions. The presence of the dogs provided needed respite for caregivers.

While Betsy was standing in line with her husband and other parents during a family orientation at the start of her oldest son's freshman year of college, a couple with two standard poodles caught her attention. She noticed that one of the dogs wore a Red Cross bandana, while the other had an identification tag that read, "Therapy Dog." Before she could strike up a conversation, three excited female college students ran up to the dogs and eagerly asked the people with them if they could pet their dogs. The couple explained that their dogs were there that day specifically to offer comfort, support, and love to anxious parents, students, and staff. After the students left, Betsy was also grateful to experience the calming effects of petting a poodle for herself, especially since it was the beginning of her son's first move away from home.

Dogs are not the only animals that can help people find moments of peace in the midst of challenging situations. Some nursing care facilities and memory centers have aviaries featuring large bird cages filled with finches and birds, as well as aquariums with fish. These indoor aviaries and aquariums bring nature inside, allowing residents, employees, and guests to observe and connect with the natural world. Research has shown that exposure to nature boosts feelings of calmness, joy, creativity, and concentration. When Betsy's children were young, her mother was living in a nursing care facility. Although she was suffering from mild dementia, she delighted in watching the birds and fish with her grandchildren. There was no past or future, only the present—only the beautiful birds, festooned with their vivid colors, flying before them, and exotic fish, a parade of beautiful movements, all of which created a sense of serenity and a shared experience.

Rehabilitation Through Caring for Animals

In the 1990s, Betsy, in the role of pastor, regularly visited a Russian prison alongside pastors and members of her church's sister congregation in Ekaterinburg, Russia. There they witnessed the rehabilitation of inmates, including working with animals as a means to attend to the men's mental health. One of the responsibilities assigned to the incarcerated men was the care of an extraordinarily large aviary which helped to bring nature into their otherwise walled-off world and provided a sense of purpose.

The responsibility given to the Russian inmates is similar to the Arkansas-based program Paws in Prison. Selected inmates train rescue dogs in basic obedience to help facilitate their adoption. By preparing these dogs to become loving, well-behaved pets, the program significantly reduces the number of animals euthanized each year. At the same time, inmate trainers acquire valuable skills that support their rehabilitation and future reintegration into society. The Arkansas Department of

Corrections has observed a positive impact on daily interactions between inmates and employees since the program began, ultimately improving security within the prison. For those involved, the presence of animals provides calm, bonding, and unconditional love where confinement, isolation, strict rules, and limited access to the outside world are the norm.

Crisis Care

When tragedy strikes—whether through natural disaster or acts of violence—therapy dogs and handlers with training from a certified organization for disaster stress relief can help provide support and comfort in highly stressful emotional situations. For example, a group known as K-9 Crisis Response traveled to Uvalde, Texas, following the devastating school shooting that happened in May 2022. Later, they returned to assist children who were coping with trauma and anxiety, offering comfort through the presence of specially trained therapy dogs.

After an EF4 tornado struck two Arkansas towns in 2014, several therapy dog handlers and their dogs—trained through our pet ministry—were called upon to assist. They were assigned to different locations to provide comfort and support. Kay, working with her therapy dog, Molly, was one of several dog handlers who along with their therapy dogs were invited to spend three days at a middle school in the town of Mayflower, Arkansas. On the final day, one young boy, whose family had lost everything in the storm, wrapped his arms around Molly's neck, looked up at Kay with a big smile, and said, "This is just the best day ever!" While unexpected tragedies create dislocation, destruction, and sometimes death, having a new non-threatening friend can reorient us to what can be good in even the most difficult seasons.

Mindfulness and Pets

Mindfulness—being fully present—is a spiritual practice, and animals often help us refocus our minds and emotions, leading to a healthier life.

After a long or difficult day, many of us return home to a pet that naturally reduces our feelings of stress—whether it's watching fish swimming in an aquarium, feeling the quiet presence of a cat curled up on the couch, or taking a walk with a dog that immerses us in the sights and sounds of a neighborhood or a park. In these moments, we are better able to let go of worries and lose ourselves in the moment. Even simple tasks we perform for our pets, such as brushing their fur or grooming them, can become a spiritual practice and a calming ritual—one that soothes both the pet and the person.

Karen Fine, a veterinarian and cancer survivor, often found herself thinking too much about what she calls "Things That Could Go Wrong." Over time and through experience, Fine learned to put her worries into proper perspective and attend to the adversity she could plan for, ultimately seeking to be present to life in the way animals are:

> I am grateful for all I have learned from animals—from watching wild animals on safari, from seeing how the lives of nomadic herders in Morocco were intertwined with those of their sheep, from connecting with people over their love for their pets, and from sharing my life with my own animal companions."[2]

In the simple presence of our animal companions and through interaction with them, we find a way to connect to the present and engage more fully with the life they are living.

When our friend Janae is working with her horse, she puts all her other concerns aside and concentrates entirely on her relationship with that horse. Horses are highly sensitive animals, quick to pick up on human emotions and stress levels. For Janae, the bond she shares with her horse has become sacred, offering her a much-needed reprieve from the pressures of daily life, including care for an elderly parent. Without this time-out, stress might otherwise consume her and take a toll on her health. To

---

2. Karen Fine, *The Other Family Doctor: A Veterinarian Explores What Animals Can Teach Us About Love, Life, and Mortality* (New York: Anchor Books, 2023), 203.

reinforce this lesson, she posted a sign outside her stable as a reminder—to herself and to those she trains—of how our equine friends teach us the spiritual practice of presence.

Mindfulness doesn't come naturally; it must be taught and practiced. Faith communities are familiar with teaching prayer, meditation, silence, fasting, or contemplative practices like *lectio divina*, a traditional method of prayer that encourages personal encounter with God through scripture. Yet there are other options to plumb the liminal or thin places where we meet the holy. Nature and animals can offer similar opportunities. In *Learning to Walk in the Dark*, Barbara Brown Taylor writes about discovering the divine in the dark or even in unlikely places we rarely think to explore. She writes of children—and we think that means adults too—that need more opportunities to allow mindfulness to seep in:

> The first few times my nephew Patrick came to see me, there was no competing with any of the handheld devices he brought with him. He was nine and loved all things virtual. If a horse could not fly and shoot fire from its nose, he was not interested in it. But he *was* interested in the green John Deere Gator parked by the garage, which was how I finally got him out of the house. Within the hour, this city kid was on his knees in the garden digging Gold Yukon potatoes with his bare hands—something he asked to do every time he came back after that, whether potatoes were in season or not.[3]

Pet ministries arise out of our desire for companionship as well as the awesome presence of the natural world, the detail in the pattern of a calico cat's fur, the silvery scales on a fish, and the abiding love of a dog who is simply glad to be.

3. Barbara Brown Taylor, *Learning to Walk in the Dark* (New York: HarperOne, 2014), 32.

Discussion Questions

1. How has your pet helped you become more present with yourself and others?
2. Stress can make it difficult to focus, and those who have experienced trauma often struggle to stay in the moment due to heightened vigilance. In what ways have you seen pets alleviate stress and trauma?
3. Programs like Paws in Prison and therapy dog visits provide comfort and healing in structured environments. How do you think these types of programs impact both the animals and the people involved?
4. Many people find mindfulness and presence through interactions with animals, whether it's petting a dog, watching birds, or caring for a horse. What specific qualities do animals have that help people cultivate mindfulness?

CHAPTER 5

Stability and Purpose

Our friend Jean has a son in medical school. When he was younger, he and his father selected a newly hatched parrot, similar to an African Grey. Now sixteen years old, Darwin remains an important part of the family, and they remain committed to his care. Though Jean's son—the bird's original caregiver—now has a demanding study load and lives nearby, Darwin still lives at home with Jean and her husband.

Since Jean has taken on the primary care of Darwin, she decided to read more about the needs of his species. For most of his life, Darwin's wings were clipped annually. Recently Jean decided to let him fully experience flight. Now, instead of hopping around on the ground, Darwin has embraced his natural abilities. He has developed an impressive wingspan and enjoys perching in various spots throughout the house—about five in total, including a wall sconce in the family's downstairs living area. He has even mastered a double turn to navigate his way upstairs. Watching him skillfully maneuver through the house delights Jean. She has come to appreciate Darwin's intelligence and his constant capacity for learning.

When the family leaves the house, Darwin often sits on the top of his cage, watching for their return through the front window. Jean is happy to accommodate Darwin's evolving needs because she sees how much happier he is when he has the ability to fly. Her family's commitment to Darwin provides him with the stability he needs as a bird with a normal lifespan of around forty years. For Jean, taking on primary responsibility for Darwin has deepened her curiosity, self-awareness, and purpose.

A recent Pew survey found that nearly all pet-owning Americans—approximately two hundred million people—think of their animals as family. According to Anna Brown of the Pew Research Center, "About half of U.S. pet owners (51%) not only consider their pets to be a part of their family but say they are as much a part of their family as a human member."[1] For some people, a pet may be their only live-in family member. These animal companions depend on their caregivers for essential needs such as feeding, toileting, grooming, veterinary care, and exercise. Caring for pets also includes planning for their well-being when traveling, whether by arranging for a petsitter, finding pet-friendly accommodations, or ensuring safe transport with seat belts or safe pet carriers. Consistency in home life and routine is also crucial for pets, and their caregivers must commit to providing this stability.

People need support, information, and opportunities to better understand the animals in their homes, and a pet ministry can help people learn what's best for their pets and foster deeper commitment to their care. A rite of passage for many children occurs when parents assign chores that include caring for a pet. For some families, taking responsibility for a pet provides a young person with a sense of purpose, an opportunity to learn about animals and their needs, and a way to develop balance through routine. Faith communities and their partners who wish to serve and support pet families can encourage these best practices and encourage responsible pet care through educational events. These might include classes on puppy socialization, guidance for working with rescued pets that have experienced trauma, and workshops on topics such as pet health and wellness.

---

1. Anna Brown, "About Half of U.S. Pet Owners Say Their Pets Are as Much a Part of Their Family as a Human Member," *Pew Research Center*, July 7, 2023, https://www.pewresearch.org/short-reads/2023/07/07/about-half-us-of-pet-owners-say-their-pets-are-as-much-a-part-of-their-family-as-a-human-member/.

During the pandemic, one of Betsy's sons, Aubrey, wanted a small pet and asked his parents for a rat. As Aubrey researched the responsibilities involved in caring for these small mammals, the family decided it was best to seek out someone who knew more about rats. Instead of purchasing a rat from a store, they reached out to a responsible breeder. Through this process, their son learned how to create the best environment for his rats, including the importance of adopting two male companions, not one solitary rat. He also discovered which toys were safe—this included avoiding exercise wheels, which can hobble a rat's feet—and learned about the essentials of proper nutrition, exercise, and other vital needs.

Dune and Coal quickly became an important part of Aubrey's daily routine. Caring for them taught him not only the responsibility of looking after another living being but also the deeper value of purpose. This experience, providing care for two animals, is what we sometimes describe as a "calling"—a responsibility that sets us apart for a specific task or ministry.

As Aubrey entered adolescence, he found even greater comfort in the companionship of his rats, allowing them to play outside their cage, crawling along his back and down his arms. Because the lifespan of rats is relatively short, their son also experienced the pain of loss. He learned that we humans can—and do—form bonds of love with even the smallest of creatures. After his rats died, the veterinary staff sent Aubrey a condolence card and ink impressions of his rats' paws and tails. This thoughtful gesture on the part of the veterinary staff honored the love Aubrey had for his rat companions and acknowledged the seriousness with which he took his responsibility to care for his pets.

Families come in many forms, often shaped by circumstances, both good and bad. Survivors of domestic violence may be hesitant to leave a dangerous and traumatic situation if a shelter does not accept their family pets. Fortunately, some designated safe havens recognize the importance of keeping the entire family together by dedicating space for the animals of families seeking protection from domestic violence. In our hometown, a well-established shelter for women, children, and some men is expanding to a new facility. The board of the shelter has intentionally made plans to house family pets, ensuring that survivors do not have to choose between their safety and their animal companions. Recognizing the reality that pets are family members fosters greater societal stability and purpose, particularly when we acknowledge the important role they play in the mental and physical well-being of so many people.

Some people need financial assistance to support their pet, and a pet ministry can help by offering resources such as food. Some low-wealth persons struggle to afford both their basic needs and the cost of caring for a pet. Yet that pet is still family. Denise, a single woman with health challenges, deeply loves her cats. In 2005, as Hurricane Katrina and the resulting flooding devastated communities, she—along with many others—witnessed the heartbreaking separation of families, including beloved pets. Beyond the human cost, countless animals were also displaced as a result of the disaster.

Moved by the news coverage, Denise approached her local church's food pantry with an idea to expand their donations to include pet food. She recognized that this would be especially helpful to the working poor and their pet family members. She knew of one elderly woman, living alone on a fixed income, who needed food security not only for herself but also for her dog. For many seniors, particularly those living alone, a pet may be their primary—or only—source of companionship.

So great was Denise's passion that she launched the initiative by raising seed money through a pet photo contest. She found a donor willing to provide dog and cat food, while her church augmented the supply with donations. One church member even asked his friends and family to give pet food in his honor rather than receiving birthday gifts, as he wanted to highlight the work being done by the pet food ministry.

Once Denise secured a steady supply of food, she distributed it monthly alongside the church's regular food pantry services. She pulled her small SUV into the area where people waited to be served, opened the hatch, and handed out bags of pet food. Perhaps the most powerful testament to this ministry was watching how many people would stand in line for pet food even before collecting food for themselves. Denise's ministry recognized the deep emotional stability and sense of purpose that pets provide people, regardless of income level. Pet ministries can support people like Denise who choose to serve pets and their families.

Discussion Questions

1. Can you recall a time in your life when a pet provided you with stability and a sense of purpose?
2. In what ways can faith communities minister to people who rely on the stability and companionship that pets provide?
3. How can pet food ministries and similar outreach programs make a difference in the lives of people facing financial hardship?
4. What are some creative ways communities can help keep pets and their families together during times of crisis, such as natural disasters or in situations of domestic violence?

CHAPTER 6

Loyalty and Devotion

Born on a farm in Japan in 1923, Hachiko was an Akita Inu adopted by Hidesaburo Ueno, a professor at the University of Tokyo. The man and the dog quickly settled into a daily routine: each morning, they walked together to the train station, where Ueno would pet Hachiko goodbye before boarding his train at the Shibuya station to go to work. Hachiko, affectionately nicknamed Hachi, would then come back to wait for Ueno's train to return.

This routine continued for sixteen months. Then, one day, Ueno did not return—he had died suddenly due to a brain hemorrhage. But how does one explain such a loss to such a loyal companion? Hachi was shuffled to several homes, always trying to return to Shibuya train station. The professor's former gardener finally took custody of Hachi. Morning and evening, Hachi continued to wait at the train station, holding his constant vigil, loyally waiting for Ueno to return. Some were annoyed by Hachi's presence, but the dog's loyalty gained national attention after a newspaper article recounted Hachi's devotion.

The Japanese people, who learned of Hachi's unwavering loyalty, were deeply moved. The dog's fidelity led to his well-known moniker "the faithful dog," and his story inspired many tributes, and even monuments, ensuring that his remarkable devotion is not forgotten.[1]

In the Hebrew Bible, the word *hesed* is frequently used to describe God's character. The term can be difficult to translate because it embodies the concepts of loyal love, enduring commitment, and faithfulness. This image of God reveals a steadfast and unwavering love—not only for humanity but for all of creation. Animals often exhibit extraordinary devotion and loyalty to those around them.

In August 2023, Rich Moore and his dog, Finney, disappeared while hiking in Colorado. Ten weeks later, the tiny Jack Russell terrier was found on Blackhead Peak, a 12,500-foot-mountain located thirty-five miles east of the nearest town—still by Moore's side. Tragically, Moore had succumbed to hypothermia.

In the midst of this crushing loss, Moore's wife, Dana Holby, found solace caring for their devoted dog. Finney had lost more than half her body weight while keeping vigil for her deceased friend. She also suffered an injury on her snout, possibly from hunting small animals to survive, or perhaps from fending off predators and scavengers. Despite everything, Finney stayed faithfully by Moore's side. Holby later expressed comfort knowing that Finney had been with her husband when he needed her most.[2]

Such steadfast care and loyalty reflect the nature of a loving God, one who walks with us through green pastures, offering provision, safety, and presence—even as we travel through the valley of the shadow when life feels dark, heavy, and threatening. This divine constancy is echoed by Paul's conviction that nothing can separate us from the love of God in Christ (Romans 8:38). The unwavering fidelity of our pets serves as a reminder

1. "The True Story of Hachiko," *BBC News*, July 1, 2023, https://www.bbc.com/news/world-asia-65259426. "Hachikō: The True Story of a Loyal Dog," *Nippon.com*, accessed May 28, 2025, https://www.nippon.com/en/japan-glances/jg00137/.
2. Caitlin O'Kane, "Miracle Dog Finney Survived 10 Weeks in Colorado Mountains after Owner Died," *CBS News*, November 17, 2023, https://www.cbsnews.com/news/finney-miracle-dog-survived-72-days-colorado-mountains-owners-death-ravenous-appetite/.

of God's faithfulness and calls us to practice deep, devoted love—not only toward one another but also in our care for the rest of creation.

Bonds with others, including our pets, are forged by individual personalities. Dedication to a relationship doesn't mean the relationship will always be easy. We grow not only from the moments of harmony but also from the bumps we encounter. Through both struggles and joys, we learn, adapt, and deepen our connections.

Ash, an English cocker spaniel, was a beloved member of Betsy's family. She had hoped he would follow in the footsteps of their previous dog, Dottie, and become a therapy dog. Ash, however, had other ideas—he saw himself as an alpha dog. Although Betsy tried to discourage his habit of sitting aloft on the family's couch cushions, atop the boys' beds, and on all the comfortable chairs in the house, Ash stubbornly insisted on his elevated thrones. When he pretended not to hear her from his lofty positions, she addressed him firmly, "Ash, come!" On rainy days, his refusal to go outside to potty was especially taxing. Still, Betsy loved him, even when his stubborn streak led to occasional snippy behavior. While biting was and is never acceptable, treats and crating helped manage his more unruly tendencies.

Ash loved his family—but he also loved food. Eating snacks, munching on ice cubes, and even rummaging through the trash can were among his favorite pastimes. In short, Ash was a pudgy handful with a big attitude. Despite his quirks, Betsy couldn't help but smile at his funny face, broad chest, wavy blue roan coat, and long ears that looked like a British barrister's traditional headpiece. Loving a difficult dog is a reminder that many of us, too, can be stubborn, in need of reformation and forgiveness. And just as Betsy accepted Ash with all his flaws, he, in turn, accepted her and her own faults.

It was odd when this food-loving dog suddenly stopped eating. At just six years old, it seemed like a temporary stomach bug or something he had eaten must have led to this unusual behavior. But it wasn't. Ash was diagnosed with intestinal lymphoma, an incurable disease. In less than a month, this once-pudgy dog had slimmed to a normal weight, and he could no longer eat. Because Ash was best friends with the family's younger golden retriever, the family's veterinarian—along with Ash's favorite vet technician and occasional pet sitter—agreed to make a house call to perform his euthanasia.

Betsy's teenage sons were given the choice to stay in the room or step away; two chose to remain, and two left. People need to be allowed to grieve in their own way. The family's other dogs remained, offering quiet companionship. Ash's vet laid out a blanket on the couch—Ash's throne and favorite place to relax. Gently placed on the soft fabric, Ash was surrounded by love as almost everyone said their final goodbyes, telling him what a wonderful dog he was. Betsy sobbed, wiping her eyes, and then apologized to the veterinarian for breaking down. He responded with compassion, "There is nothing better that you could give your dog than to be with him to the end as he has been faithful to you." What remains for Betsy now are the memories of a unique bond—a relationship that required patience, understanding, and a willingness to embrace Ash's peculiarities, including his absolute devotion to her.

Animals are not only devoted to us but also to one another. Years ago, Betsy read a book that deepened her appreciation of animal emotions. *When Elephants Weep: The Emotional Lives of Animals* is more than just a study of animal emotions, it is also filled with stories. The book recounts remarkable instances of animal emotions across species. For instance, learning that elephants hold rituals for their lost loved ones offered new insights to Betsy and reshaped her understanding of how grief affects the animals in our homes.

One of the most helpful pet ministry programs offered by our friends at Resurrection United Methodist Church in Leawood, Kansas, provides ongoing education about animals and their emotional lives. One notable program featured guest speaker, Barbara J. King, author of *How Animals Grieve.* As an anthropologist at the forefront of understanding animal emotions, King's research has helped people recognize grieving behavior found in animals, allowing humans to be more present for them—just as they are present for us.

Grief is a natural response to the loss of those we love and toward whom we feel deep devotion. A powerful example of this came into public view in 2018, when the world witnessed an orca mother, Tahlequah, mourning the loss of her calf. She carried the lifeless baby for seventeen days, nudging it, holding it aloft, and gripping its tiny fin with her teeth. Though Tahlequah subsequently gave birth to a healthy male in 2020, she suffered another heartbreaking loss in 2024, once again holding onto her deceased calf. Her closely knit pod of female orcas remained by her side, demonstrating a level of support and solidarity that mirrors our own expressions of grief. [3]

A growing body of research suggests that many non-human animals display profound care for one another, offering comfort, loyalty, and even acts of mourning—reminding us that love and loss transcend species. We can learn from their devotion and loyalty.

Discussion Questions

1. Living with a devoted and beloved pet often deepens our sense of commitment, teaching us to walk with them through good and bad times. How can having a pet with strong-willed or unruly characteristics help us learn the values of dedication and patience?
2. Have you ever shared your life with an uncommonly loyal pet? How did their devotion change you? In what ways did it shape your perspective or change your life?
3. Animals have been observed grieving for their lost companions, as seen in cases like Tahlequah the orca. How do these examples of animal grief change the way we think about the emotional lives of animals?

---

3. Mindy Weisberger, "Orca Mother Tahlequah Seen Carrying Dead Calf Again," *CNN*, January 7, 2025, https://www.cnn.com/2025/01/07/science/orca-carrying-dead-calf-tahlequah. Lynda V. Mapes, "Mother Orca Tahlequah Once Again Carries Her Dead Calf," *The Seattle Times*, January 5, 2025, https://www.seattletimes.com/seattle-news/climate-lab/mother-orca-tahlequah-once-again-carrying-her-dead-calf/.

4. Pet loss can be deeply painful, and many people find comfort in knowing their pets were surrounded by love in their final moments. How can individuals and communities better support those grieving the loss of a beloved pet?

CHAPTER 7

Reading the Room

Domestic animals that live with us often provide support in ways that go beyond our primary senses. Some animals even have an innate ability to assess the mood or atmosphere of a group by picking up on subtle, nonverbal cues—ranging from body language to facial expressions.

Certified therapy dogs visit a variety of institutional settings and are quite good at reading and responding to human emotions. There are structured programs to help children develop their reading skills by allowing them to read aloud to a certified therapy dog. Thesc therapy dogs instinctively pay attention to facial expressions, tone of voice, and body language, creating a nonjudgmental and encouraging environment for young readers.

Jeri Haynie and her therapy dog, Brandy, visit the youth floor of a local public library each week. There, Brandy—fondly known as the Library Dog—curls up on her pillow, ready to listen attentively or receive a pat or a hug. Among Brandy's devoted fans are Samantha, Olivia, and Jeremiah, who eagerly rush to see her each week. They read to her, draw pictures of her, and love to watch her do tricks—especially her signature paw wave.

Brandy also visits special needs classrooms at a local high school. When she was first introduced to Miss Katherine's class, the teacher encouraged Jeri to accompany Brandy wherever her therapy dog wanted to go. Without hesitation, Brandy made her way to sit under the chair of a girl who wore plastic gloves because of her fear of touch. Jeri was quite apprehensive about Brandy getting too close to the girl, but the teacher came over and gently helped the girl pet Brandy. The teacher reassured her by describing how soft the fur felt. Reluctantly, the girl reached out and touched Brandy for the first time—a small but significant step toward overcoming her fear. When Brandy returned for her next visit, the girl had made remarkable progress: she no longer wore gloves.

In *Vision: A Memoir of Blindness and Justice*, David S. Tatel, a retired judge who served in the United States Court of Appeals for more than twenty-three years, shares the story of his early struggles with retinal disease, first diagnosed when he was only fifteen years old. For many years, he tried to hide his condition, adapting to a world of increasing darkness. Despite his visual impairment, he built a highly successful career on the bench. Eventually, he began using a cane, which signaled his disability to others, allowing them to offer additional support when needed.

In 2019, Tatel received his first guide dog, Vixen. Not one to openly discuss his blindness, he soon discovered that having Vixen by his side transformed his experience. The dog liberated him, empowering him to talk more comfortably about his blindness. Not only did Vixen provide the judge with greater independence, but her presence also invited people into conversation—giving them a natural way to engage with Tatel. In turn, this helped him form connections with people he might not have otherwise interacted with. He humorously remarked that if talking about one's dog is a crime, he would plead guilty.[1]

Horses, too, offer emotional insights and profound lessons about how to overcome challenges when working with others. Working with horses can also help people better understand their own behavior, improve

1. Jacey Fortin, "Judge David S. Tatel on Vision, Blindness and the Supreme Court," *New York Times*, May 27, 2024, https://www.nytimes.com/2024/05/27/us/david-tatel-vision-blindness-supreme-court.html

communication skills, and develop trust and cooperation. In an article for *The New York Times Magazine*, Sterry Butcher describes horses as "exquisite machines" and then adds:

> As prey animals, their greatest survival tools are designed for flight, and every sense is finely geared toward safety. In the wild, they spend the entirety of their lives within the eyesight of another horse . . . They can see nearly 360 degrees and can focus on two objects at once, one from each eye . . . Their hide is so sensitive to the touch that they can feel a single fly land on their body and wriggle the skin underneath to send it aloft. Their sense of smell is almost as keen as a dog's.[2]

Because a horse's heightened sensitivity is honed to its self-preservation, interspecies communication with them is especially complex. Butcher points out that some trainers today are steering away from obedience-based training toward approaches built on mutual trust and cooperation. Rather than forcing submission, these methods encourage a deeper, more intuitive relationship—one in which horses help humans learn more about ourselves and how we adapt our behavior to build stronger, more understanding connections with one another as well. Horse trainers now appreciate how well a horse reads the corral. We humans are better with our pets when we read the room the best we can when they're in it.

Horses are not alone in providing us with this kind of opportunity for introspection. As humans, our insight and awareness are limited. We miss social cues, struggle to communicate effectively with one another, and often fail to read the room. Moreover, we often struggle to perceive and understand the perspectives of others. In contrast, animals frequently possess heightened abilities that we lack, making them valuable guides in helping us better understand ourselves and one another.

---

2. Sterry Butcher, "What Warwick Schiller Teaches About Horses—and People," *New York Times Magazine*, November 12, 2024, https://www.nytimes.com/2024/11/12/magazine/warwick-schiller-horses.html.

Some years ago, Betsy and her kids watched the documentary *My Octopus Teacher*, the true story of Craig Foster who began daily freediving in a kelp forest off the coast of Cape Town, South Africa. The film documents Foster's developing relationship with an octopus, whom he follows for almost a year. He bonds with her and learns how she lives, eats, sleeps, and defends herself from predators. It's a beautiful story and a moving documentary that features an animal in the wild who mentors the man observing her—helping him learn more about himself and enabling him to forge a closer relationship with his son.

Animals can also be our spiritual guides. Fr. Richard Rohr suggests that, although we call ourselves intelligent, we have lost touch with the natural world—which, in turn, has distanced us from our own souls. When that happens, he writes, "I believe we can't access our full intelligence and wisdom without some real connection to nature!"[3]

Animals teach us to pay close attention to the details of the good creation all around us. They help us become more attuned to signals and information from others we might otherwise overlook.

Discussion Questions

1. Have you ever experienced a greater awareness about yourself or others through the perspective of a domestic animal? What insights did you find most helpful?
2. In the Christian tradition, we seek ways to grow in love for God and our neighbors. How can ministry with animals help us become more compassionate, connected, and loving?
3. Animals often perceive things that humans overlook, such as emotions, social cues, or environmental changes. How might paying closer attention to animal behavior help us become more attuned to the needs of others?

3. Richard Rohr, *The Soul, the Natural World, and What Is* (Albuquerque, NM: Center for Action and Contemplation, 2009), MP3 audio.

4. Many people have found spiritual wisdom and guidance through their relationships with animals. Can you think of a time when an animal taught you something meaningful about faith, patience, or resilience?

PART TWO

For the Love of Neighbors

"Perhaps once we can see God in plants and animals, we might learn to see God in our neighbors. And then we might learn to love the world."
—Fr. Richard Rohr[1]

"[Red] came to help guide me and lead me to higher ground—to hospice work, the Mansion [assisted care facility], the refugees. He helped me to do good and to learn how to love doing good because Red could go anywhere, be anywhere, see anyone. Because of him, so could I."
—Jon Katz[2]

1. Richard Rohr, "Contemplating Creation," *Center for Action and Contemplation*, October 10, 2021, https://cac.org/daily-meditations/contemplating-creation-2021-10-10/.
2. Jon Katz, "Red Came to Lead Me to Higher Ground," *Bedlam Farm Journal*, August 9, 2019, https://www.bedlamfarm.com/2019/08/09/red-came-to-lead-me-to-higher-ground/.

CHAPTER 8

Animals and People: Creating Community

Several years ago, we all experienced a collective trauma—we survived a pandemic that dramatically altered the way we live. Stuck in our homes, some of them filled—or overfilled—with family, pets became anchors for many amid an uncertain world. They soothed our loneliness and anxiety and provided us with an opportunity to disconnect, even if just for a few moments, from the terrors and frustrations beyond our doors.

The soothing presence of an animal is also featured in the story of Saint Roch, a thirteenth-century pilgrim and caregiver who became the patron saint of dogs. Roch, a wealthy young man from France, was said to have been born with a red cross on his chest. After losing his parents, he devoted his life to Christ, giving away his inheritance to help the poor.

During a spiritual pilgrimage in northern Italy, Roch encountered the devastation wrought by the bubonic plague. Instead of fleeing in horror, Roch stayed and cared for the sick. As could only be expected, Roch eventually contracted the plague himself. Not wanting to burden others or risk infecting them, he retreated to the forest to die alone. However, this was not to be his fate.

Some versions of this story say that Roch had taken his family dog with him on the pilgrimage, while others claim that a stray dog found him during his time of need. Regardless of the version, this dog aided him in his recovery. According to legend, the dog licked his wounds, helping them heal, and brought him bread daily to sustain him. When times are tough, when we need healing, from illness or heavy circumstances that weigh us down, caring for one another may not only create community but sustain it.

At the beginning of the creation story in Genesis, there's a beautiful depiction of God's provision and abundance for all life. As God makes the entire world, an opportunity for community emerges, taking root in the fertile ecosystem of a garden. In that garden, God places a human and observes aloud, "It's not good that the human is alone" (Gen. 2:18).

This divine observation acknowledges the fundamental human need for companionship and community. In response, God creates the creeping things, the wild animals, the birds in the sky, and the domesticated animals, but even then, God is not finished.

One of the clear intentions for creation is community—not superficial relationships, but deep, meaningful connections. God creates another human, a companion from the earth, one who carries the same essence as the original form. Both are crafted from the dust of the ground and are called to care for one another and the rest of creation. Within this divine plan, humans are also entrusted with the responsibility of nurturing companionship throughout creation.

However, we are a long way from that perfect garden where everyone has enough—enough love, compassion, resources, and support. Modern societal and technological trends often encourage division, judgment, loneliness, and isolation, rather than the meaningful relationships that help us grow and thrive. As we continue to adjust to this world with its easy technological distractions and temptation toward self-isolation, people struggle to find balance and community between home, family, and work. Many have found that their social skills have diminished, making it more difficult to connect with others.

In addition, the scar tissue of COVID-19 remains for many. Educators have noted dramatic shifts among Generation Z, often referred to as "Gen P" for "pandemic," referencing the increased social disruption they experienced during a formative time in their lives. The shift to online learning during COVID-19 significantly reduced opportunities for interpersonal interactions, leading to weakened communication skills among many students in that age cohort.

A 2021 survey conducted by the Survey Center for American Life revealed that our social landscape has become much less conducive to creating strong communities. The authors cite lower marriage rates, declining religious involvement, and increased workplace disconnection as major contributors. A rise in virtual interactions—Zoom meetings, webinars, and social media—combined with poor urban planning has made it harder for people to form and sustain friendships. As a result, Americans have experienced a massive decline in close friendships, a phenomenon researchers have called the "friendship recession." This shift has led to reduced community engagement, volunteerism, and civic participation.[1]

In recent decades, the word "religion" has become a stand-in for closed-mindedness, anti-science, and uncompromising beliefs. However, the Latin root word, *religare*, means to bind or connect, more specifically it means to reconnect. At its core, any religious tradition can create opportunities for deep connection and community between people, enriching our quality of life. In a time when we need each other more than ever, we must be intentional about fostering relationships. Yet, in the busyness of daily life, we can easily overlook essential values of relationship building—such as respect, play, hospitality, teamwork, and shared experiences.

Pets, however, offer us unique pathways to engage more fully with one another, helping us forge deeper connections in ways we might not expect.

---

1. Daniel A. Cox, "America's 'Friendship Recession' Is Weakening Civic Life," *Survey Center on American Life*, August 24, 2023, https://www.americansurveycenter.org/newsletter/americas-friendship-recession-is-weakening-civic-life/.

One of our favorite places is Parnassus Books, an independent bookstore in Nashville, Tennessee. Parnassus Books is owned by author Ann Patchett and is known not just for their carefully curated selection of books, but also for their shop dogs, who greet visitors as they browse. For book lovers like us, this store can feel like a cathedral—a sacred space that celebrates the spiritual practice of reading. In our view, having dogs in a bookstore elevates it to the status of a shrine. (For all the cat lovers, Betsy also once adopted two cats from an Episcopalian bookstore.)

Ann Patchett chronicles the journey of the shop dogs in her delightful book *The Shop Dogs of Parnassus*. The first shop dogs were Lexington, a dachshund, belonging to the store's first events director, and Sparky, a rescue dog who belonged to Patchett. In keeping with the bookstore's commitment to literacy and outreach, all proceeds from the book benefit the Parnassus Books Foundation, which provides books to schools and underserved communities.

Gayle and Betsy reached out to Sarah Arnold, Parnassus Books' marketing director, to learn more about the shop dogs and how they help create community in the store. Arnold said,

> The shop dogs are definitely a morale booster for our staff. We all bond over playing with the dogs and getting to laugh with them. Even when the store is busy and everything feels overwhelming, it's hard to take things too seriously when a puppy is squeaking a toy behind you—they put things into perspective. Sometimes we forget to take breaks, and the dogs are a helpful reminder to pause, eat a snack, and step outside.

Beyond providing a calming presence for those working in the store, the shop dogs also extend hospitality to customers. Arnold added, "People come into the store asking for the shop dogs all the time—often it's folks from out of town, sometimes it's local college kids who miss their dogs at home, or parents who are appeasing a dogless child. People are usually very happy to see the shop dogs."

For those uncomfortable around dogs, the store posts a sign on the door, letting visitors know that if they're afraid of dogs, they need only notify one of the booksellers, and the dogs can be put in the backroom.

It's not just people who come to see the shop dogs either. Other dogs are welcome too! As long as visiting dogs are leashed and well-behaved, they're welcome to come inside. Some have even become regulars, like a sweet pit bull mix who always wears a fun outfit.

Parnassus Books has fully embraced the joy and community-building power of its shop dogs, hosting special events such as a canine commitment ceremony, a *Where's Waldo* Day, where the dogs dress up in costume, and a mayoral race between the shop dogs. The bookstore's beloved dogs are featured on some of the store merchandise like t-shirts and stickers.

Word gets around quickly when a place is welcoming, and relationships built on this mutual kindness tend to flourish. Barnabus, Sarah Arnold's dog, formed a longstanding bond with the shop's FedEx delivery driver because the man always carried Milk-Bone snacks and gave Barnabus a treat with every delivery. However, when the route changed and a new driver took over, he arrived empty-handed. Barnabus never forgave him. Even after weeks passed, Barnabus continued barking at him, making it clear that he hadn't forgotten the missing treats.

One fall day, our own love of pets and books came together in a meaningful way when our church hosted an animal blessing with a children's literacy emphasis. As part of the event, we invited Paper Hearts, a pop-up bookstore, to set up in the parking lot, asking them to bring a wide selection of children's books. We encouraged church members and guests to buy one book to donate to a local school, ensuring that the event not only celebrated the bond between people and animals but also helped the children in the community around us.

Pets can serve as natural icebreakers, helping people communicate and connect more easily and deeply. They can also inspire creative ways to serve our neighbors, whether by supporting school children in need of books and encouragement to read more, or bringing companionship to those experiencing loneliness.

Discussion Questions

1. How do pets help foster connections between people? Can you think of a time when an animal helped you start or strengthen a relationship?
2. The story of Barnabus and the FedEx driver highlights how animals remember acts of kindness (or the lack thereof). What does this tell us about the importance of consistency and care in our relationships—with both animals and people?
3. In what ways can events like an animal blessing or a pet-friendly gathering be used to build stronger community ties? How might such events be adapted to serve different groups of people?
4. Pets are natural icebreakers. How can we use our relationships with animals to encourage hospitality, kindness, and outreach in our communities?

CHAPTER 9

Compassion and Mercy

One evening, Betsy's oldest son was walking in Washington, D.C., where he attends college. He sent a picture and a very brief video to the family chat. The photo was striking—a vivid image of a barred owl, a large striped bird of prey. From the sound of his voice in the video, we could tell that he had not expected to see such a wild creature in the heart of the D.C. metropolitan area. His tone was filled with absolute awe as he basked in the imposing presence of the spectacular bird, perched on a big branch, staring right at him. We could hear his surprise, mixed with reverence, the kind of respect elicited when we encounter something wholly different than us. This interaction with a wild animal was special and beautiful, but not all our exchanges with animals go well. Some of our relationships with animals require compassion and mercy.

We live in a time when the guardrails of social decorum and genuine affection seem to be eroding, leading to a decline in trust between one another. Too often, we forget that all people—not just those in our own in-group—desire to be valued and appreciated. How we treat animals can serve as a barometer of what we truly value and how we tend one another.

A stark example of both neglect and compassion surfaced in the aftermath of Hurricane Milton in Florida, when a viral photo and accompanying story captured national attention. The Florida Highway Patrol posted a video on social media showing a dog that had been abandoned, left tethered to a pole as floodwaters quickly rose around him. State officials had adamantly urged people to bring their pets with them to shelters set up specifically for pet families, thus ensuring their safety during the storm. Yet despite these warnings, someone had left the dog, a bull terrier, behind to face the rising waters alone.

By the time the troopers arrived, the water had reached the top of the dog's legs. The officers rescued the dog—now named Trooper in honor of his rescuers—and took him to a veterinarian to make certain he was unharmed.[1]

The public response to social media posts about the dog's abandonment was swift and emotional. Animal advocates and pet lovers were outraged by Trooper's neglect, particularly during a deadly storm. His story, however, became a powerful reminder of not only the unacceptable aspects in human behavior, but also the best—highlighting the importance of respect and responsibility toward animals entrusted to our care.

Once Trooper was placed in the safe keeping of the Leon County Humane Society, many families applied to adopt him. He appeared nervous with some of the prospective families, but thankfully he found a home with Frank and Carla Spina, a couple who have a long history with the breed and already had Dallas, another bull terrier. Dallas had been grieving the loss of the couples' other dog, who had died earlier that year. The moment Trooper met Frank and Carla, he seemed at ease. And when he was introduced to Dallas, the connection between the two dogs was immediate.

The Leon County Humane Society shared Trooper's story to remind people that countless animals are in need of rescue. They emphasized the importance of valuing and caring for animals, ensuring they are placed

---

1. Wendy Grossman Kantor, "Trooper! Florida Highway Patrol Rescues Dog Tied to Pole Before Hurricane Milton Makes Landfall," *People*, September 9, 2023, https://people.com/florida-highway-patrol-rescues-dog-tied-pole-before-hurricane-milton-makes-landfall-8726086.

in homes where they are loved, respected, and their needs are fully met. Trooper's story not only highlighted the importance of rescue—it also led the Florida Legislature to pass "Trooper's Law," a new reform that makes restraining and abandoning a dog during a natural disaster a third-degree felony. This painful story and others like it remind us that pet ministries can partner to work on important, life-saving legislation for the humane and ethical treatment of animals. It's difficult to comprehend why anyone would tie up a dog in deadly storm, but animal welfare advocates need solutions that prevent such harmful decisions—like offering shelters that accommodate pets.

Of course, there are many stories that teach us similar lessons about respect that fosters compassion. In *Saving Simon: How a Rescue Donkey Taught Me the Meaning of Compassion*, Jon Katz recounts his experience rescuing a severely abused donkey and bringing him to live on his farm. After developing a deep bond with Simon and helping him to heal, Katz made an unexpected decision—to visit the farmer who had been fined for neglecting the donkey.

Katz had no desire to confront the man or condemn him, as he realized that he didn't know the man's story or his circumstances. Katz, however, was largely alone in that position. Many people who heard about Simon's mistreatment were quick to judge the farmer harshly. Instead, Katz reflected on the basic definition of mercy, which is forbearance shown to another who has suffered, is vulnerable, or has made an awful mistake. Katz decided to lean into compassion, uncertain of the man's situation and unable to judge him only on Simon's obvious neglect.

When Katz met with the farmer responsible for Simon's neglect, he learned his farm had been struggling for years. The farm was failing, and he had never wanted the donkey—Simon had come as part of a package deal when the farmer acquired horses that he needed. By the time Katz visited him, the man was barely able to feed his horses or his own family. He had become so defeated and worn down that he was past caring what anyone thought of him.

While Katz did not excuse the farmer's neglect, he wondered why so few people seemed concerned about individuals like this man—people so overlooked and devalued that no one saw them as worthy of compassion and respect.[2]

Compassion is a hallmark of Jesus' ministry, evident in many stories where Jesus ministers to marginalized and diverse people he viewed as neighbors. Some of the most merciful and respectful expressions of his ministry involved compassion for and healing of the sick and outsiders, what we animal lovers might call "strays." When people suffer from physical or mental illness, the pain extends beyond the individual, affecting their families, communities, and hurting everyone involved. Illnesses consume money, time, and emotional energy—a reality that has remained unchanged for over two millennia.

Another central aspect of Jesus' ministry was hospitality and sustenance. He shared meals with anyone and everyone, not just with those he knew or liked, but with those who were hungry—both physically and spiritually. His actions demonstrated universal respect and compassion, a model for those who follow him.

In recent years, wildfires, especially in California, have forced families and their pets from their homes, leaving them in urgent need of shelter and rehoming. As fires and the resulting destruction spread faster and into more populated areas, mass evacuations—often carried out within minutes—have become increasingly common.

Caitlin Doran grew up in the Pacific Palisades area, in a home that was just a few doors down from her grandparents' house where her mother was raised. Her aunt and uncle also lived nearby. Caitlin had raised her twenty-three-year-old African tortoise, Tiptoe, in that house after asking Santa for the unique pet when she was just seven years old. Back then, he fit in the palm of her hand.

2. Jon Katz, *Saving Simon: How a Rescue Donkey Taught Me the Meaning of Compassion* (New York: Random House, 2015), chap. 10, "The Farmer," 95–105.

As fire engulfed her old neighborhood, it became clear that none of these beloved family homes would survive the fire, so Caitlin and her boyfriend sprang into action. They evacuated the entire extended family to her rental home in Marina del Rey. In the very small house, Doran managed to shelter all eleven adults, along with three pit bulls, one Labrador, one cat, and her beloved 175-pound tortoise, Tiptoe—though the tight quarters made it especially difficult for the animals. By day's end, Doran's landlord sent over a work crew to build a safe, outside enclosure for Tiptoe and the other animals, allowing greater freedom and less confinement. As climate change intensifies, natural disasters are becoming more frequent and severe, forcing us to reconsider how we care and make room for those who suffer catastrophic loss—including our pets.

Recovery and Rehoming

Issues of addiction and substance abuse are often lower on the list of priorities when it comes to funding decisions, despite the urgent need for access to treatment and resources. Many of those who struggle with substance abuse are unable to get the support they need, in part due to stigma and negative biases within society. Many of these individuals are also caregivers—not just for family members, but also for their pets. In some cases, a pet is their only source of companionship and family. Faith communities should take note.

Thankfully, there are groups that strive to provide assistance to those who are struggling with addiction as well as their pets. Each year, CNN honors individuals and organizations that make extraordinary contributions to humanitarian aid and make a difference in their communities. The 2024 recipient of this recognition was Dogs Matter, an organization dedicated to assisting individuals in addiction recovery while ensuring the well-being of their pets. The stated mission of Dogs Matter is, "To provide and promote a safe and healthy environment for pets of recovering addicts and alcoholics."[3]

This unique rescue program respects the critical bond between people who need treatment and their animals, recognizing that this relationship can be a powerful motivator in the sobriety process. The nonprofit provides foster homes and veterinary care for pets while their primary caregiver receives treatment, ensuring that both humans and animals receive the care they need.

Finding people who understand the commitment and responsibility required to properly care for a pet can be difficult. Providing for a domestic animal involves more than just food and shelter—it also includes nutrition, exercise, training, and medical care.

Mona, an advocate for shelter rescue, dedicates her time to helping animals find safe homes. She is passionate about reducing shelter overcrowding and often reminds people of the importance of respect and long-term commitment when adopting a pet.

Recently, she shared on social media a frustrating reality she encountered at one of the shelters she works with: Five dogs were adopted in a single week—only for each of them to be returned the next week. The reasons? Everything ranging from hyperactivity to potty training issues to the adoptive pet parent's belief that the dog simply didn't like their new surroundings.

In her post, Mona reminded people that domestic animals need more than a week to adjust and become part of the family. Dogs, especially those coming from shelters or traumatic backgrounds, need a calm, quiet environment and a consistent routine to feel safe.

This includes following the 3-3-3 rule for rehoming, a general guideline for helping dogs adjust to a new home. The rule outlines three key stages of transition: 1) the first three days are used to adjust to a new environment, 2) the first three weeks are best for bonding and training, and 3) the first three months are meant for further training and socialization.

---

3. Dogs Matter, "Our Mission," accessed May 29, 2025, https://dogsmatter2.org.

We never know what kind of trauma an animal or a person has experienced. We can only know what we witness in behavior. Animals, especially those who have had a traumatic or chaotic life, remind us that we need to respect every person and every life and take the necessary steps to healing and wholeness that support our neighbors who need help.

Discussion Questions

1. What does our treatment of animals reveal about our capacity for compassion toward people?
2. How might a pet ministry be an extension of Jesus' teachings on mercy, healing, and hospitality?
3. What lessons can we learn from stories like Trooper the dog or Simon the donkey about both judgment and mercy?
4. In what ways could a pet ministry respond to modern challenges—such as natural disasters, homelessness, or addiction—while embodying the values of the gospel?

CHAPTER 10

Play

Children are wired for play—it's how they explore and make sense of the world. Yet as we grow up, many of us forget the importance of play and neglect to make time for it. We get caught up in responsibilities, schedules, and routines, losing sight of the fact that we need play—not just for fun, but to build personal connections and to experience the precious emotional rewards that follow.

Fortunately, when we have a pet in the home, we are constantly reminded of the joy of play. Unlike humans, animals never seem to outgrow their desire to play, move, and have fun.

Play is vital for a pet's physical and mental well-being. Having a pet encourages spontaneous, voluntary, pleasurable, and joyful activities. Play also allows us to get a break from the clock and enjoy the moment. It even offers us a natural way to stay active and get in better physical shape.

Ever had a dog bring you a toy? Ever seen a dog's face light up when you pick up their leash to go on a walk together? Ever had a bird fly to your hand and start talking? Ever watched a cat leap after a feather teaser? Then you have seen and experienced the joys and rewards of play.

Betsy's young golden retriever, Paddington, is named after the charming and beloved British bear of children's literature. Much like his namesake, Paddington is polite, kind-hearted, and always eager to please. However, he also has an endless capacity for getting into innocent mischief, though he tries so hard to get things right.

Along with his golden bear-like face that inspired his name, Paddy's personality matches the famous bear's charm. He is playful, affectionate, and adorably clumsy. His infectious enthusiasm for play has spread through their entire household. Throughout the day, family members find themselves picking up Paddy's favorite toys—a stuffed bone, donut, or a dinosaur—and throwing them down the hallway for him to chase. While fetch is one of his favorite pastimes, like most golden retrievers, he is just as excited to simply bring them a wadded-up paper towel or hand towel that had been left on the floor. He is always eager to help in his own way. He does try to get things right.

Whenever Paddy plays, Betsy and her family can't help but smile, laugh or both. His enthusiasm for play often makes playtime a spontaneous thing, but this innate desire is also an important reminder that pet parents should set aside intentional playtime in addition to these moments of spontaneity. These intentional moments are important ways to support a pet's physical health, mental well-being, and socialization skills. These are the same reasons that humans need to set aside time to play too. Time for play should be considered a spiritual exercise as well, one faith communities can support.

Places and Types of Play

Varieties of play and physical activity are essential. Many people have access to safe walking areas, public parks, or designated dog parks, where pets can exercise and socialize. For pet families looking for more private or specialized spaces, there are rentable dog parks, like those offered by Sniffspot. These pay-per-use parks provide a safe and secure environment, ideal for a pet family that is traveling or those looking for an exclusive space for playdates, exercise, or special events. These parks, rented out by private owners, may include fully fenced areas, water features, hiking trails, or agility courses.[1]

Beyond casual play, there are also more structured activities in which dogs and their handlers can train. These specific activities, which involve work but also play, provide both exercise and mental stimulation. They require dedication and teamwork but also serve as exciting forms of play.

Think about training and participating in friendly competitions of agility, nose work, and dock diving. Agility is a competitive sport in which dogs compete to navigate an obstacle course while maintaining proper speed and alignment. (While commonly associated with dogs, cat shows also often include tests of agility!) Canine nose work is a growing activity where dogs are trained to detect and locate a scent hidden in various locations. Dock diving is a high-energy sport that helps improve a dog's agility, health, and weight management by encouraging them to leap from a platform into the water to retrieve a toy.

Activities like these strengthen the bond between a pet and their caregiver while providing an opportunity for physical exercise, mental engagement, and social interaction. Whether through a casual walk or competitive training, play remains a central part of an animal's well-being.

Play as a Social Connector

Play can also be an important part of social gatherings, especially in communities that encourage pet participation. Many cities now feature pet-friendly spaces that foster interaction and companionship—both for animals and their humans. In the city of Fayetteville, Arkansas, the Good Dog Cafe is a restaurant designed for dog lovers and their pets. The cafe was the dream of two dog lovers who envisioned a space where dogs

1. For some pet parents, access to specialized parks and play areas is a luxury. Some even struggle with basic necessities such as collars and leashes, and finding safe spaces to walk their dogs can be a challenge. It's important for those involved in pet ministry to be mindful of socio-economic factors and remain aware of the struggles some might face regarding mobility, convenience, and cost when caring for their pets.

could play safely while their caregivers enjoyed good company. To bring this vision to life, they custom-built obstacles and play structures on a grassy yard, giving energetic dogs a place to have safe adventures, burn some energy, and play with friends. The owners describe how the cafe has evolved beyond just a dining space:

> The cafe's become a community. We know almost every dog's name when they come through the door. People really recognize each other and become friends. People aren't on their cell phones, they are talking and laughing and having a good time. That's what makes it special, people are coming together.[2]

And it's not only the people who are socializing—the animals are too. Some pet-friendly eateries not only encourage bringing your dog, but also find ways to observe special days and host celebrations. In our area, a dog-friendly gathering space called Bark Bar celebrates National Dog Day on August 26, offering nutritious dog treats and pup-cakes in special recognition of all the dogs that bring joy and companionship to our lives.

Cats and Community

While dogs may be more commonly associated with playtime, other animals require play as well. However, we may not always think about structured play for them or for ourselves. Cats often carry a stereotype of being solitary creatures, and those with cats may be perceived the same way. But cats and cat lovers do, in fact, crave play and find their own ways to connect and engage with one another.

Betsy's family has two cats, Cougar and Tiffany—one social, one shy. They enjoy playing with feather toys, hiding in boxes, and leaping from shelf to shelf. We know some feline families build "catios"—enclosed outdoor patios that allow their cats to safely observe and experience the outdoors.

---

2. "Good Dog Cafe: Where Pets and People Play," *About You: Arkansas Lifestyle Magazine*, August 2023, 60.

Beyond the home, cat lovers gather at cat-friendly cafes, where they can enjoy coffee, socialize, and participate in cat-themed activities. Others engage through organized gatherings of registered breeders, such as The International Cat Association (TICA) or the American Cat Fanciers Association (ACFA). These events foster a sense of community, welcoming both purebred and non-purebred cats. Some cat groups also sponsor agility exhibitions, grooming workshops, photography sessions, as well as educational information from feline experts.

This kind of official gathering also creates room for human connections and play. At one local cat show, several rescue organizations were present, using the event as a platform to advocate for animals in need. A close friend of ours adopted a cat at the event—a feline survivor of intentional cruelty, recovering from gunshot wounds.

Hearing stories like these encourages empathy and action. Spaces where people gather with their pets don't just create opportunities for play and fun—they also raise awareness about animal welfare and encourage advocacy for animals in need.

Our local zoo, which is accredited by the Association of Zoos and Aquariums (AZA), has long provided an opportunity for children of any age to learn about and observe animals. Visitors can explore a wide variety of different species, their unique behavior, and how they live and play.

In the twenty-first century, accredited zoos are held to high standards of animal care. They are no longer merely for entertainment but also provide support for global conservation efforts and maintain programs focused on species survival. It's encouraging to see how much thought and effort goes into animal care, and this includes opportunities for play.

During Betsy's travels, her family has always looked for AZA-accredited zoos and discovered the many ways zoos offer different animals ways to play, think, work, and interact. These zoos recognize that animals need stimulation, exercise, and play to thrive, not merely food and shelter. When her family visits, they often discover a wide variety of toys and objects of play that have been provided for the animals. The careful attention paid to the needs of these non-domesticated animals reminds us that humans are not the only species that want and need play. Play is a fundamental part of life.

Discussion Questions

1. What does it mean to think of play as a form of care for both pets and people?
2. How can your church or community be mindful of the socio-economic realities and challenges of providing for a pet? Do you have free space to provide play for people and their pets?
3. What opportunities for connection—between people and between animals—are created when we center play? How can your community provide space for these opportunities?
4. How do stories like Paddington's reflect the heart of Christian faith and mission?

CHAPTER 11

Welcoming Spaces

Betsy's boys enjoy taking one of their adventurous cats outdoors on a leash. This supervised exploration is important not only for the cat's stimulation and safety but also because Betsy's husband, Victor, is an avid birder. He is careful to ensure that the cats do not attempt to disturb or hunt wild birds. While the birds are not pets, they are part of creation, and he enjoys observing their behaviors, migrations, and interactions. However, when the boys take the cat outside, everyone gets to enjoy this welcoming space in harmony.

Similarly, one of our young friends, Emery, takes her cats on adventures in a see-through backpack, allowing them to experience the world beyond their home while they remain safe and secure. This kind of creative exploration with her cats enables the animals to engage with their surroundings while also deepening their relationship.

Creating Welcoming Spaces

Intentionally building and shaping welcoming spaces is an important part of Christian hospitality. This practice of welcoming is not only true for people, but for pets as well. When we create these hospitable, secure spaces they serve to foster community and connection.

During COVID-19, our small church organized an outdoor event in our parking lot called "Dogs in the Woods." The lot borders a wooded area, and we invited everyone to bring their own pop-up chairs and pets. We set up fire pits throughout the parking lot and had several people working the grill, preparing hot dogs. Since several new people had joined our congregation via our online ministry, it also provided an opportunity for them to attend and connect in person. It was a wonderful time to be together outside in the cool weather and get to know the pets and the people in our faith community.

Beyond our own community, we've noticed an increasing number of businesses that welcome pets inside their spaces, including art galleries, farmers' markets, and well-known retail stores, such as Bass Pro Shops, Tractor Supply, Michael's, L.L.Bean, and Pottery Barn.

In our town, a popular brewery and restaurant called Southern Tail makes pet-friendly spaces a core part of their business, offering indoor and outside spaces for pets and their people. They offer movie and trivia nights, but some of the best play is on the enormous patio where dogs and people participate in yoga and corn hole. For those inclined, fun includes such occasions as celebrating Dolly Parton's birthday in costume. Their outdoor pub is designed as "a haven where you can relax, indulge in delicious craft beer, and build lasting connections with our community."[1] Beyond simply welcoming pets, they also work with local nonprofit organizations to support nonprofits benefiting animals.

Our local minor league baseball park, Dickey-Stephens Park, home of the Arkansas Travelers, sponsors an annual Dog Night, bringing together baseball fans and dog lovers for a fun pet-friendly evening. The park is also home to a resident grounds dog, Dizzy, who is listed on the club's website as the official "Ballpark Pup." Dizzy, whose owner is park superintendent Greg Johnston, has become a beloved mascot for the team. She is so popular that she has her own line of bobbleheads, baseball cards, and

1. Southern Tail Brewing Co., "Home," accessed May 29, 2025, https://www.southerntailbrewing.com/.

mini-plush toys, making her as much a part of the game-day experience as the players themselves. This openness and encouragement of integrating pets into the experience of the park makes the games a more welcoming environment for everyone.

As church folks, we believe that gathering outside of traditional church settings is essential for learning more about our communities and the needs of those within them. By creating welcoming spaces for both people and animals, we foster deeper connections, encourage inclusivity, and strengthen relationships in meaningful ways.

Welcoming Spaces in Faith Communities

Within Christian communities, several seasonal events help to create welcoming places for pet people to gather. Many churches observe the Feast of St. Francis of Assisi in October, an occasion that celebrates the saint's well-known love for animals and provides an opportunity to bless the animals of those who attend.

In her work as a pastor and celebrant at these events, Betsy has blessed every kind of animal from dogs, cats, rabbits, and turtles to a bearded dragon named Hazel. Hazel was the much-adored bearded dragon of a local preschool class. She received her blessing while fully clothed in a remarkably trendy outfit. Betsy has also had the opportunity to bless a family's sick hen, who arrived at the blessing in her own coop. At the time, the chicken was experiencing eye issues, which can be quite serious. Not long after the blessing, the devoted pet parent joyfully shared that the hen's eye had miraculously healed.

Events like these are not limited to a spiritual experience. They also offer a way for people to connect with each other over their shared love of their pets, finding common ground, even if only for a short period of time.

Some faith communities, like College Mound United Methodist in Terrell, Texas, offer the regular presence of rescue dogs who help greet worshipers. Members bring treats for these gentle dogs, some of whom remain for the worship service. A friend who preached at the church noted that the county shelters are chronically overfilled, and this church offers a way to support animals in need of homes. The special occasion for these pets and people is simply gathering for weekly worship.

Community Through Partnership

Beyond faith-based gatherings, relationships with nonprofit organizations, veterinary clinics, and pet advocacy groups can provide valuable opportunities to learn about and support pet families. Activities and events that welcome pets and teach about pets can bring people together, fostering their shared love of animals.

Stephanie, the manager of a local urgent care veterinary clinic, reached out to ask us what we were doing for World Pet Memorial Day, an annual observance recognized by the American Veterinary Medical Association. She encouraged our pet ministry to offer a special service for people who had lost their pets during the previous year.

Although this observance was new to us, we embraced it and began planning an event to honor and remember beloved pets. We initially wanted to hold the gathering in a community location like a public park, but ultimately decided on the quiet, garden-like space behind our church, adjacent to a wooded area. We wanted this to be a simple, yet meaningful ceremony incorporating an interactive ritual for healing. We invited attendees to bring pictures for a Pet Memory Table where they could display photos of their beloved pets. To spread the word, we designed promotional graphics, made yard signs and placed them around the community, used social media, and sent out press releases. Stephanie also notified all the local veterinary offices and shared the event online.

On the day of the event, we weren't sure what to expect. We arranged folding chairs so people could casually pull up a chair as they gathered on the church grounds. At the appointed time, cars began to pull into the parking lot—then more, and more. In total, fifty people, most of whom we had never met before, gathered together to honor their pets' memories. Attendees carefully placed their cherished photos on the Pet Memory

Table, which quickly became a beautiful display of love and remembrance. Among the tributes were framed pictures, photo albums, professionally painted portraits, and family Christmas cards that featured the now-departed pets.

As everyone came together, a guitarist played, creating a peaceful and reflective atmosphere. To begin the ceremony, Gayle read a passage about caring for creation and the significance of animals in our lives, emphasizing that pets are family. Stephanie then spoke about her experience working in a veterinary urgent care facility, sharing the emotional challenges of helping families say goodbye to their pets. She described how staff members provide support during these difficult moments, acknowledging that losing a pet is not only painful for the families but also for the caregivers who treat them. Being there every day, through these tough times, the clinicians know exactly how much people love their pets.

Karen Fine, in her book *The Other Family Doctor: A Veterinarian Explores What Animals Can Teach Us About Love, Life, and Mortality*, reflects on the emotional weight of performing euthanasia on someone's pet—many of whom are suffering or nearing the end of their lives already. Although it is an immensely difficult duty, Fine approaches it with a spiritual perspective, viewing it as an ethically honorable task. It's what her mother called a *mitzvah*, "a Hebrew word meaning a good deed, a sacred duty in the Jewish faith."[2]

Following Stephanie's heartfelt witness at the memorial event, we invited everyone to turn on the flashlight on their phones, hold them high, and say the name of their pets aloud, one by one. To conclude the ceremony, Betsy offered a blessing over the pictures and mementos that people had brought to honor their pets. It was a tearful time, yet also a powerful and healing experience. Strangers came together to form a community, bound by shared love and loss, each remembering a special pet who had touched their lives.

---

2. Karen Fine, *The Other Family Doctor: A Veterinarian Explores What Animals Can Teach Us About Love, Life, and Mortality* (New York: Anchor Books, 2023), 167.

Throughout the event, we had meaningful conversations with several attendees about their particular pet, learning each pet's name, how they became part of the family, and the unique stories that made them special. These intimate moments revealed a deep need for communal grief support for those who have lost a pet.

Many people long for space to talk about their deceased pets, to share what they miss, and to be with others who understand this loss and the palpable grief that comes with it. This grief can be just as profound as losing a human loved one, often manifesting in sleeplessness, loss of appetite, and even depression.

Remember Betsy's son and his two pet rats? When their tumors progressed, her husband took them to be euthanized—a sad but necessary act of mercy. This was difficult not only for their son but also for her husband, who had witnessed the special bond between the boy and his beloved pets.

The loss of a family pet must be validated, especially by spiritual communities. Congregational care leaders in churches, synagogues, mosques, and other faith communities should consider offering resources to provide grief support and spaces for people who want and need to gather together to share their loss and honor their pets.

Providing a safe and compassionate space for people to mourn their pets can be a powerful way for communities to extend care and healing to those navigating this very real and deeply felt loss.

Discussion Questions

1. What does it mean to create a welcoming space for all of God's creatures—both human and animal—in our church community?
2. In what ways can events centered around animals (like blessing, memorials, or pet-friendly gatherings) deepen relationships within and beyond the church?
3. How does recognizing and honoring pet loss challenge or expand our church's understanding of grief and pastoral care?

4. What partnerships—with veterinarians, shelters, local businesses, or other organizations—could help your community become a hub for compassionate, creative, and inclusive pet ministry?

CHAPTER 12

Teamwork

Pam is a professional dog trainer and a certified nose work instructor. She uses methods from the National Association of Canine Scent Work and has entered her dogs in competitions where they search for specific scents such as birch, anise, clove, cypress, vetiver, and myrrh.

Recognizing a growing need in her local schools to detect vape products, Pam decided to train her seven-year-old German shepherd, Immix, to locate these banned items. Through classical conditioning methods, Immix learned to identify nicotine along with related scents. Within a few weeks, he was successfully finding vape canisters that Pam had hidden in various locations, including the local Lowe's store.

Not long after, Pam and Immix had an unexpected encounter. While Pam held the door open for a woman at a hotel, Immix suddenly stuck his nose deep into the woman's large purse. Embarrassed, Pam quickly apologized, but the woman laughed at the incident. Curious about what triggered Immix's reaction, Pam asked her new acquaintance if she happened to be carrying any nicotine products. The woman confirmed that she had a vape pen in her bag.

While the two women found the moment humorous, it reinforced how the serious scent work Immix had been trained to perform could now help Pam detect vape products in local schools

Pam also serves as a professional who helps us test our church's therapy dogs. All dogs must pass a test with a certifying organization. We've learned that all sorts of persons with expertise and varied skills and backgrounds can come alongside those who want to do pet ministry and create teams that seek greater communal good.

The Power of Community and Teamwork

In our faith tradition, we prioritize building diverse communities, working together, and helping those in need. At our best, we incarnate love in action. Jesus intentionally formed a community of people with diverse backgrounds and temperaments. They all had flaws, but they also all belonged. As difficult as it may have been for a tax collector and a nationalistic zealot to get along, that's the model we see in the Gospels.

Jesus also called people with various types of occupations and callings. His community included everyone from fishermen to tax collectors to women, who also helped support his ministry financially. Jesus frequently reminded his followers that their calling included serving in the world by using their unique gifts. Many of us live and even work with our cherished, distinctive pets, and sometimes our animals are part of shared, work communities.

Humans and animals have been working alongside one another for thousands of years. In fact, dogs were the first domesticated animals. Science journalist Ed Yong reflects on this saying, "We [humans] raised puppies well before we raised kittens or chickens; before we herded cows, goats, pigs, and sheep; before we planted rice, wheat, barley, and corn; before we remade the world."[1]

---

1. Ed Yong, "A New Origin Story for Dogs," *The Atlantic*, June 2, 2016, https://www.theatlantic.com/science/archive/2016/06/the-origin-of-dogs/484976/.

This working relationship between humans and animals has benefited society in numerous ways, offering protection, service, tracking, farming, stress reduction, and even message delivery. Carrier pigeons played a vital role in communication before modern technology. Likewise, dogs have been natural alarm systems, alerting humans to potential threats with their barking. Cats helped with the elimination of rodents and decreased the spread of disease, though we might want to keep that fact a secret from our beloved pet rats!

Animals with Jobs

Humans continue to work alongside animals and many domestic animals today have essential jobs. Under the Americans with Disabilities Act, service animals—including dogs, and occasionally miniature horses—are trained to assist individuals with vision, hearing, and mobility impairments, as well as those living with chronic illnesses, psychiatric conditions, or life-threatening medical issues such as diabetes and seizures.

One inspiring example comes from the life of Grace Mariani, a young college graduate who uses a wheelchair due to cerebral palsy, a condition she was diagnosed with after being born prematurely at just over twenty-four weeks. Despite the challenges she faced, Mariani pursued her education with fervor, always accompanied by her loyal service dog, Justin—a yellow Labrador–golden retriever mix.

When Mariani crossed the graduation stage to receive her college diploma, Justin was right by her side, just as he had been in every class throughout her academic journey. As the college president handed Mariani her diploma, he also presented a special diploma for Justin, who gently accepted it in his mouth, wagging his tail and to the cheers of the entire auditorium. This moment is a beautiful reminder of the unbreakable bond between humans and their working animals.

Together, as a team, Grace Mariani and her service dog, Justin, made it possible for her to accomplish her goal of becoming a special education teacher for children with intellectual disabilities. But Mariani doesn't teach alone—Justin is part of the team.

Mariani's accomplishment was not accidental; it was the result of years of specialized, intensive training provided by Canine Companions, an organization founded by Charles Schulz, the creator of the Peanuts comic strip and the famous beagle, Snoopy. Today, Canine Companions is a leading provider of service dogs for adults, children, and veterans with disabilities, as well as for healthcare, criminal justice, and educational settings. Their number one core value is teamwork.

Building Trust

Early in his ministry, United Methodist Bishop Warner Brown served the Western Pennsylvania Conference as both a pastor and director of social service ministry. During his time, he worked with junior high school students who were learning how to groom and care for horses before taking them on a safe ride, also known as "walking the horse." Brown accompanied the students through their training, understanding the unique role horses can play in learning, personal growth, and team development due to their keen instincts and sensitivity to human emotions.

Later in his career, Bishop Brown was assigned to be the episcopal leader of the Rocky Mountain Conference. He was aware of existing tensions between the district superintendents who served on the bishop's cabinet and the Board of Ordained Ministry. His goal was to build trust between these two groups, and to do so, he introduced them to equine-assisted learning.

The purpose of this exercise was to foster teamwork, with the ultimate goal of safely getting their leader—the bishop—on the horse. Because horses are highly sensitive to human emotions, the team had to act in complete harmony to approach the horse and to assist the bishop in riding bareback: there would be no blanket, saddle or reins. Bishop Brown described the teamwork to include keeping him on the horse as the group walked beside him and the horse, guided only by his verbal instructions on what he needed to stay calm and feel secure. At the same time, the bishop also had to fully trust his team with his own well-being and safety.

It took effort, communication, and cooperation, but the group eventually came together as a unified team—one that was now ready to work collaboratively in the service of others. In that moment, Brown knew with certainty that his team had his back. The exercise had succeeded where traditional team-building activities had failed, proving that true collaboration is built through shared experiences, trust, and mutual reliance.

For years Brown kept a picture of the horse that helped unify his ministry team on his desk, with a designated title for this special animal: My Coach.

Discussion Questions

1. How do the stories in this chapter expand your understanding of teamwork—not just among people, but between people and animals? In what ways might pet ministry become a space where spiritual and emotional partnerships between animals and humans are honored and supported?
2. What does it look like for the church to affirm the many "jobs" animals do—both formal and informal—in people's lives? How might recognizing animals' contributions shape our ministries with children, veterans, people with disabilities, or those experiencing mental health challenges?
3. Bishop Brown's story highlights how equine-assisted learning can build trust and improve collaboration. How might your church or small group use shared experiences with animals to build deeper trust and community?
4. What role can your community play in advocating for and supporting those who depend on emotional support animals or service animals? Are there ways your community can better welcome, accommodate, or minister to individuals whose well-being is shaped by their animal companions?

I AM A THERAPY DOG
Therapy Dogs
Give People
and Joy.
dogs greeting you
hello.
WOOFMAS

CHAPTER 13

Animal Ambassadors

We like to imagine that Jesus took his dog to work. We have no proof that Jesus even had a dog, but Jesus lived in a world where animals were part of everyday life and labor. Luke says that Jesus, in his first moments of life, was wrapped in swaddling cloths, and placed in a manger—an ancient feeding trough for animals. Although we don't know whether Jesus was born in a stable, an adjacent but crowded guest room, or a cave, we know he was born in Bethlehem, near animals.

We also know that shepherds guarding their flocks are an important part of the nativity story—and those shepherds likely had herding dogs. Shepherds in Bethlehem were tasked with birthing lambs for temple sacrifice, and the lambs were wrapped in cloth to protect them from injury, then laid in feeding troughs. Perhaps that's why Luke wants us to notice a connection between Jesus and a lamb—both a vulnerable creature, both a sacrifice for the world.

While there are minimal references to dogs in the Gospels, we enjoy leaning into the Jewish interpretive practice of midrash, an ancient interpretive practice in which rabbis "reimagine dominant narrative readings while crafting new ones to stand alongside–not replace–former readings.

Midrash also asks questions of the text; sometimes it provides answers, sometimes it leaves the reader to answer the questions."[1]

Scripture challenges us to use our imagination, as seen in the many adaptations of biblical stories into films and even television shows—like *The Chosen*—which portrays Jesus through the eyes of those who knew him best and wrote the Gospels. Each episode allows for fresh interpretations, including one in which Jesus, before beginning his public ministry, demonstrates his carpentry skills by crafting toys for local children while telling them the stories of Israel.

Keeping in this tradition, let's think about dogs. In scripture, dogs don't have the best reputation. To call someone a "dog" is meant as an insult. In Matthew 15:21-28, the story of the Canaanite woman illustrates this. While Jesus is ministering in Tyre and Sidon, north of his home in Galilee, a woman from that region approaches him and shouts her need for help *at* Jesus. She begs him to heal her daughter. At first, he ignores her. As she continues pleading, the disciples grow irritated by her tenacity. But she will not stop. She is relentless in her pleas.

Finally, Jesus responds, telling her that his ministry is meant for the lost sheep of the house of Israel. Nevertheless, she continues to ask, insist, and beg—like, well, a dog. Jesus says it isn't right to throw the children's bread to the dogs, reinforcing her status as an outsider. But the woman does not back down. She boldly replies that even the dogs eat the crumbs that fall from their master's table. With that, the woman changes the narrative and the trajectory of the conversation. Jesus acknowledges her faith and grants her request, expanding his ministry to include those beyond the original flock. The table expands and those once called "dogs" are now invited to the communal feast.

Faith communities can be notoriously slow to accept change, even positive change. We should also note how measured humans can be when taking in new information in other settings, whether business, education,

1. Wilda C. Gafney, *Womanist Midrash: A Reintroduction to the Women of the Torah and the Throne* (Louisville, KY: Westminster John Knox Press, 2017).

government, or cultural institutions. In our midrash from Matthew's Gospel, Jesus shows us that we can learn "new tricks," and sometimes the best way to do so is to experience an ambassador, like that Canaanite woman, who can champion a new path, a new ministry.

As we've already said, working with nonprofits is one way to develop a pet ministry. When Betsy's children were in preschool, she became involved with a foundation that helped raise funds to create a penguin habitat at the local AZA-accredited zoo. While we understand that some people find zoos to be inhumane, AZA zoos and aquariums are highly regulated, provide species conservation funding, and follow practices that support wildlife survival—an especially important mission in our rapidly changing climate.

Because of this newly planned project for penguins, school children were able to learn through the visits of "ambassador" penguins. With the help of trained handlers, these penguins went to "work" at schools as part of a Pennies for Penguins program, teaching younger children about the environment, climate, habitat, and species diversity—while also raising funds for the habitat. The children's interaction with the penguins brought the stories in picture books to life, helping them feel more connected and empowered to care for both domestic and tame or wild animals.

Something similar happens when teachers keep pets in the classroom—snakes, rats, bearded dragons, hamsters, or other small animals or reptiles. These animals serve as visible, daily learning opportunities in a public space. Classroom pets can enrich learning across subjects. For example, math lessons may involve weighing the rat, while science units may explore where an animal comes from or what it eats. Writing prompts might ask students to describe the pet's appearance or behavior.

Beyond academics, classroom pets teach children to be more aware of the needs of others—human and animal alike. When students are involved in feeding, cleaning up after, and interacting with animals in school settings, they begin to understand that all living creatures require care and attention beyond food and water. Students also learn how their behavior and actions affect others. Studies indicate that animals in the classroom may help improve social skills such as cooperation, communication, and empathy in the learning environment and reduce anxiety.[2] That's one reason we love it when our therapy dogs visit schools—they bring calm, joy, and connection into spaces where they're most needed. Additionally, faith communities might choose to support pets in the classroom by assisting educators with the care and support of classroom animals.

One of the more visible examples of animal ambassadors who go to work with their handlers are dogs in K-9 units. These canines are an integral part of the police force. These dogs are often trained to patrol and track, and they live with a designated handler—becoming part of the handler's family, just like any other dog. When they are off-duty, police dogs enjoy the same activities other pets do: walking, hiking, playing, and simply relaxing at home.

Gayle once observed this special bond firsthand at a restaurant where an off-duty police officer, still in uniform, was working security. She noticed his SUV nearby, designated as a K-9 patrol vehicle, and asked the officer if his dog lived with him. With great pride, he pulled out his phone to show her pictures of his German shorthaired pointer, the dog's official K-9 identification, and he proudly bragged about his friend and partner. These dogs are not just tools for law enforcement—they are family members and ambassadors for their departments, often joining their handlers at school functions, scout troop visits, and regular public and civic appearances.

Other animal ambassadors may represent a business or organization's acknowledgment of the deep bonds we share with our pets. Increasingly, companies like Replacements, Ltd. are gaining attention for their pet-friendly policies. Replacements, which specializes in connecting people with discontinued china, glassware, and flatware, is regularly recognized

---

2. "Pets in the Classroom: What Are the Social, Behavioral, and Academic Effects of Classroom Pets for Children 8–10 Years?," *Human Animal Bond Research Institute*, accessed May 29, 2025, https://habri.org/grants/projects/pets-in-the-classroom-what-are-the-social-behavioral-and-academic-effects-of-classroom-pets-for-children-8-10-years.

as one of the most pet-welcoming workplaces in the country. The company's mission is rooted in preserving memories or family traditions, stating that they're in the business of passing on cherished pieces for "another lifetime of voices, stories, laughter, and love."[3]

Their website even features a section dedicated to their "Pet Family," which includes the pets that employees bring to work. The team's cohesion is enhanced by the presence of their "furry co-workers." The company posts videos on its website about events they observe together, like National Love Your Pet Day.

And they are not alone! Eleven percent of employers now allow dogs to come to work.

When we speak of beginning a pet ministry in faith communities, we offer ideas that involve pet family care, education, or animal advocacy. Yet faith communities contain persons who go to work and serve the public in a variety of vocations with their animals. Churches and other faith communities should give consideration to the ways people share their lives with animals beyond our own settings and spaces. It is important to equip and encourage individuals who may want to serve with their pet in a unique ministry through their work life.

In our United Methodist Christian tradition, our founder, John Wesley, understood that ministry to others did not stop with a single congregation or parish or boundary. Because he saw the world as his place to serve all God's children, he often ministered far and wide traveling by horseback an estimated 250,000 miles. That is a lot of time spent at work and in ministry with his horse.

---

3. Replacements, Ltd., "Why Us," accessed May 29, 2025, https://www.replacements.com/why-us.

Discussion Questions

1. What can we learn from Jesus' willingness to expand the boundaries of his ministry in response to unexpected voices—like the Canaanite woman? How might this story guide us in making space for animals and their caregivers in the life of the church?
2. How do animals serve as "ambassadors" in human spaces—schools, workplaces, police forces, zoos, and ministries? What might be the spiritual or pastoral role of animals in our own faith community?
3. In what ways could a pet ministry mirror the work of ambassador animals—offering connection, education, calm, or healing to those inside and outside our church? What unique opportunities might pets create for outreach, hospitality, or community support?
4. If animals were part of the everyday world Jesus inhabited, how might we reimagine discipleship, church life, or pastoral care in light of this? How could a ministry that honors animals help us live out our call to steward creation and extend hospitality to all?

CHAPTER 14

Loving Underdogs

Nori is turning gray. She's a liver-and-white German shorthaired pointer, and Betsy's family adopted her when she was about a year old. Betsy saw her on a local rescue site and fell in love with the vulnerability she saw in Nori's eyes.

Nori was found and rescued by a woman near local Lake Norrell, hence her name, Nori, which was given by her rescuer. Though she comes from a naturally lean breed, Nori was emaciated and covered in fleas and ticks when she was rescued, but she was already on the road to recovery the day she was welcomed to her new home. Nevertheless, there were other struggles. She had anxiety and chewed the edges of the couch. She was a runner who would bolt through doors if the family wasn't careful—something common in high-energy hunting breeds like hers. Nori also has always been protective of her legs and feet, perhaps due to past mistreatment that still remains with her to this day. After she settled in, Betsy had a trainer come in to help with her behavior. Over time, Nori became one of the family and is also their longest-living dog. Now a senior, she spends more time sleeping, but she still enjoys a walk and a tug-of-war with her friend Paddy. She also has become the favorite of the extended family, inspiring Betsy's brother to paint a portrait of her that now hangs prominently in the kitchen

Each one of us is unique, and every animal is unique as well. Just as humans have individual, identifiable fingerprints that belong only to a single person, dogs also have completely unique features, nose prints to be precise. Yet despite this individuality and uniqueness, dogs also share 99.9 percent of their DNA with their wolf ancestors. It's the same with us. While we can now access our own diverse ancestry, discovering that we are a mix of many different ethnicities and peoples—we are all still human at our core.

In our Christian tradition, some theological perspectives suggest that the incarnation of God in Christ represents the meeting of the spiritual and material worlds, and that in Christ all things are reconciled (see Col. 1). Christ's body is a transformed material body, one that allows God to share Godself with all of creation—from worms and snakes to animals, birds, flowers, and seeds. This deep unity in the Christ of all creation is what inspired St. Francis to refer to all creatures as "brother" or "sister." We believe all beings have their origin in the creating and redeeming love of God in Christ. That also means that, like Jesus, we pay extra attention to the needs of the underdogs among us. Pet ministries can educate humans in learning to love what some would discard as unattractive or not useful.

Unfortunately, and too often, we make judgments based on external appearances—how someone or something looks. Left behind in this cycle are the animals perceived as less desirable—the outsiders, the strays. Just as people hold biases and prejudices toward other people who are different, the same holds true for animals, including pets. One striking example is the phenomenon known as Black Dog and Cat Syndrome. Statistically, black dogs and cats are adopted from shelters far less frequently than lighter-colored animals. This trend appears to stem from outdated superstitions—like the belief that black cats bring bad luck—and is reinforced by portrayals in media, where black animals are often cast as sinister or dangerous. Likewise, human villains frequently wear black, reinforcing this negative association.

As observed in the documentary *Inside a Dog's Mind*, historically many dog breeds developed and thrived primarily to suit the preferences of people with higher social status and not because of their specific task-oriented traits. Instead of flaunting a designer purse or fashionable clothing, some people displayed particular types of dogs to signify their rank or sense of refinement. This trend continues today with the relative rise and fall in popularity of certain dog and cat breeds.

Another common prejudice we humans have is directed toward large-breed dogs such as rottweilers, mastiffs, and German shepherds. People often assume that adopting these breeds will be more expensive due to higher veterinary bills and higher cost of food. There is also a widespread assumption that these breeds are more aggressive. However, many large breeds are actually quite calm and mellow by nature, often requiring less exercise and fewer potty breaks than their smaller counterparts.

According to the American Society for the Prevention of Cruelty to Animals (ASPCA), approximately 2.7 million animals are euthanized in shelters each year—1.2 million dogs and 1.4 million cats. About two out of every five of the dogs euthanized are pit bulls, a breed that has developed a reputation for aggression. This stereotype persists even though pit bulls were historically affectionately referred to as "nanny dogs" for their gentle and calm disposition around children.

Another group of often-overlooked animals are elderly pets. Judging a pet based on graying fur, cloudy eyes, reduced energy, or even incontinence is a form of ageism, mirroring society's attitudes toward aging humans. Yet the commitment required to care for an older pet is often shorter in duration. We previously mentioned our retired friend Stacy, who regularly adopts hospice dogs—pets that are elderly and who aren't expected to live much longer. Stacy views her care for these dogs as a personal statement about how she wants to be treated as she ages—she relates to their aging process and models the kind of care she hopes to receive.

Betsy and her husband, Victor, experienced something similar when they adopted Daisy, her mother's elderly dog. After moving into an apartment, Betsy's mother could no longer care for Daisy. At first, Daisy seemed frail. But with regular walks and socialization with their other dogs, she became more active, lost weight, and rediscovered a playful spirit. She ended up living another three years. Victor, who had insisted on taking care of Daisy to reassure Betsy's mom, later joked, "We were duped. That dog was not on her last leg!" Despite the joke, we knew we had rescued an underdog.

At an adoption event organized by a church Betsy was serving, she and two friends were observing all the adoptable pets. Among them was a solid black dog—a small Labrador mix—with a noticeable issue affecting her back legs. By the end of the event, the dog was still unclaimed and available for adoption. Mary, one of Betsy's friends, couldn't stand the thought of this dog being left behind simply because of her color and disability. She adopted her on the spot. The dog was named "Lily," and the meaning was clear: this dog was a flower—beautiful in spirit, with a lovely heart, regardless of the color of her fur or her physical limitations. Lily and Mary shared many good years together. Lily turned out to be an excellent passenger in the car, happily accompanying Mary almost everywhere she went.

Faith communities can educate people about the importance of adoption of those who are cast aside, the underdogs. We can teach how Jesus demonstrated and taught, to care for the least of these (Matt. 25:31-46). Veterinarians and their staff understand this well. Karen Fine notes, "assorted pets of veterinary clinic staff are typically some combination of one-eyed, three-legged, partially paralyzed, diabetic, [and] behavior-challenged" animals.[1]

Betsy's first English cocker spaniel, Riley, was adopted from a breeder after being returned by two other families. One family said they were too

1. Karen Fine, *The Other Family Doctor: A Veterinarian Explores What Animals Can Teach Us About Love, Life, and Mortality* (New York: Anchor Books, 2023), 182–83.

busy, and the second—a couple navigating a cancer diagnosis—could no longer manage his care. In the midst of this shuffle, Riley was overfed and became overweight. The breeder helped him slim down, but later Riley developed pancreatitis and eventually diabetes.

His worsening condition required daily care: Betsy had to take him out first thing in the morning and catch his urine on an insulin strip, then give his injection for the day. Riley only lived four more years, but he left a big impression. He growled when we scratched his chest, a vocal quirk that quickly became endearing: it was simply his way of talking! He loved walking and, like Ash, another cocker spaniel in Betsy's life, Riley was into pillows—the more elevated, the better. Early in Betsy's marriage, Victor complained about Riley lying on his bed pillow. Innocently, Betsy replied, "But Sweetie, he was bred for pillows!" Riley's life began as a potential show dog, but his early families couldn't care for him and returned him. Yet Betsy gained a wonderful companion, and she can testify to how caring for under-valued animals can be a deeply spiritual experience.

There is no disability, no age, no color, no gender, no illness, and no difference that can separate us from divine love—no condition is beyond God's care or ours. Our intimate relationships with animals call us to love the outsider and care for the underdog—the ones who are rejected or who might be discarded. These bonds with our pets can deepen our spiritual practice of radical acceptance and inclusion. They remind us not to judge others because they are different from us and encourage us to prioritize love in both our attitudes and actions.

Discussion Questions

1. How do the stories of animals like Nori, Lily, and Riley challenge the way we think about value, beauty, and worth in both animals and people? In what ways does caring for "underdogs" reflect the heart of the Gospel?

2. This chapter draws a parallel between bias against certain animals and the way we judge people. How might pet ministry help us confront our own assumptions or prejudices? How can loving overlooked animals become a spiritual practice of radical acceptance?
3. What does it mean to say that "no condition is beyond God's care or ours"? How could your church or ministry embody this truth, especially in the way it includes aging, disabled, or misunderstood animals and the people who love them?
4. Many of these adoption stories involve second chances, healing, and transformation. How could your community become a place where those stories are celebrated for animals and people alike?

PART THREE

A Field Guide for Creating Pet Ministries

"The more you open to connection, the more you get. The more you believe you are worthy of connection, the more connection appears in your life."
—Jon Katz[1]

"God of the sparrow
God of the whale
God of the swirling stars
How does the creature say Awe
How does the creature say Praise"[2]

1. Jon Katz, *Saving Simon: How a Rescue Donkey Taught Me the Meaning of Compassion* (New York: Random House, 2015).
2. Jaroslav J. Vajda, "God of the Sparrow, God of the Whale," *The United Methodist Hymnal*, music by Carl F. Schalk (Nashville, TN: The United Methodist Publishing House, 1983), 123.

HYMNAL

CHAPTER 15

Why Communities Should Consider a Pet Ministry

Our church campus is located near Pinnacle Mountain State Park. Its beauty attracts large numbers of people who bike, hike, walk, climb, and visit because they love being in nature. We humans are animals, part of nature ourselves. That's one reason it never surprises us when people say they feel closest to God—or the divine or the sacred—while outdoors. Some even tell us they have no need to go to church or participate in a religious community because of their time communing with God in nature.

The sad part of that sentiment is that Christians should know and reclaim, both in our theology and our practice, a deep sense of awe and reverence for the incredible creation of God. We need to recover the witness that all creation praises God. All we have to do is look at the psalms of praise—music from the creation itself—many of which describe how the whole world resounds together in worship: mountains, oceans, and animals alike. Christians are part of the whole creation community, not simply a group inside a building.

Over time and through a variety of experiences, we've realized the need for a ministry with neighbors who have companion animals, including those not affiliated with a faith community. Regardless of their spiritual background, anyone can participate in pet ministry for the good of creation—for the animals and the people who love them.

Swift Social Changes

Not that long ago, most people kept pets outdoors, within their fenced yards, and didn't allow them into our homes. Today, that practice has mostly faded. For most people, our pets are members of our families. If our dogs or cats aren't sleeping in our beds, they're certainly sleeping under our roofs.

When an EF4 tornado hit the northwest part of our state of Arkansas, one survivor recounted placing her seven cats in the bathtub—their designated safe place. They were not left outside to fend for themselves. They were family and you don't leave family to endure that alone.

We've redefined what family means.

We are not the only ones to notice this societal shift. As we've already mentioned, a growing number of retailers and businesses have acknowledged the role of pets in our families by creating products in areas like clothing, bedding, transportation, accommodations, nutrition, and play that fulfill the desire to integrate pets more deeply into our lives. This trend only seemed to accelerate after the pandemic, a time when people spent significantly more time at home with their pets.

Statistics vary, but it is clear that in the U.S., we have more pets in our households than children.[1] More than half of those who have pets are Millennial women (ages 29-44). Additionally, one-third of the women in that generational cohort are religiously unaffiliated and choosing to have children later.[2] The U.S. birth rate recently reached a low not seen in more than three decades.

---

1. Forbes Advisor, "Pet Ownership Statistics," accessed May 29, 2025, https://www.forbes.com/advisor/pet-insurance/pet-ownership-statistics/.
2. Kinship Partners, "Millennials Choosing Pets Over Kids," accessed May 29, 2025, https://www.kinship.com/pet-lifestyle/millennials-choosing-pets-over-kids.

The generation behind the Millennials, Gen Z (ages 13-28), also tends to say they'd rather have a pet than a child, though their attitudes and preferences may change over time. Thirty-four percent of Gen Z is religiously unaffiliated.[3]

These statistics help explain why Americans, including Christians, spent $136.8 billion on pets in 2022 and are projected to spend $157 billion in 2025. You can even see this shift reflected in home design, with features created specifically for pet families. Examples include dog showers and tubs, built-in feeding stations with pot fillers to keep water fresh, bookshelves designed for feline exploration and play, and furniture that cleverly conceals litter boxes or promotes inconspicuous indoor pet living.[4]

As "church ladies" with a passion for our pets, we want faith communities to do more for people and their animal companions. At the same time, we, along with many other faith leaders, can see that attendance and participation in churches have been steadily declining for years, a decline that accelerated during and after the pandemic. There are a number of reasons people cite for not seeking religious affiliation, including judgmental attitudes from Christians, partisan politics, prejudice, insularity, frequent appeals for money, and, for some, the simple joy of being in nature instead of sitting inside a building.

Yet something has been lost. Generational shifts and the decline in church attendance and affiliation have created a vacuum, with fewer opportunities for organized spiritual community. In our area, a private Facebook group for women often becomes a place where members seek advice or recommendations on everything from healthcare and educational resources to catering services and communities of faith. Regularly, anonymous posts appear from women requesting safe, inclusive communities of faith where LGBTQIA+ families will find a real welcome. Others express a longing for spaces where their children—and they themselves—can

3. Public Religion Research Institute, "Generation Z: Fact Sheet," accessed May 29, 2025, https://www.prri.org/spotlight/prri-generation-z-fact-sheet/.

4. Capital One Shopping, "Pet Spending Statistics," accessed May 29, 2025, https://capitaloneshopping.com/research/pet-spending-statistics.

grow morally and spiritually, but without the baggage or harm they associate with a traditional church experience.

We can see that many of these women carry deep wounds. As children, teens or young adults, they were silenced, harmed, or conditioned not to ask questions. As a result, they now perceive most organized communities of faith as lacking in authentic relationships, transparency, and the freedom to question while still feeling safe and included. We suspect many of them also could not imagine churches welcoming their pets.

Unmet Societal Needs

John Wesley, the founder of the Methodist movement, did not confine himself within the walls of a church building. We feel sure he would have recognized and embraced new ways of creating "fresh expressions" of community. That's because he went where the people were ignored and hurting—ministering to the elderly, the poor, those struggling with class divides, the incarcerated, the uneducated children, and those working dangerous jobs like miners.

Recognizing these human needs, Wesley traveled more than 250,000 miles on horseback, bringing the good news of God's love to those marginalized by society and the staid Church of England. His horse wasn't merely a mode of transportation—it was his valued, trusted companion. Wesley believed so deeply in that bond and God's love for all creation that he suggested his horse would join him in the resurrection.[5] And, in the first *Book of Discipline* published by the Methodists, eighteenth-century circuit-riding preachers were advised to ensure that their horses were well-cared for: "Be merciful to your Beast. Not only ride moderately, but see with your own eyes that your horse is rubbed and fed."[6]

---

5. John Wesley, "The General Deliverance," in *The Sermons of John Wesley*, 1872 edition, accessed May 29, 2025, https://wesley.nnu.edu/john-wesley/the-sermons-of-john-wesley-1872-edition/sermon-60-the-general-deliverance/.

6. *The Book of Discipline of the Methodist Church*, 1784, accessed via Christian History Institute, https://christianhistoryinstitute.org/uploaded/50cf81cc64f6c0.60843690.pdf.

Wesley's travels and his commitment to forming new small groups helped people find connection and belonging, overcoming isolation and building a movement rooted in love and care. We think Wesley would have embraced this "new trick," this new inclusion of pets as a sign of our spiritual care for God's creation and one another.

One way to respond to folks' desire for community and connection is to broaden our understanding of community—especially those of us who are in religious spaces—by recognizing the vital role pets play in the lives of most of our neighbors. These neighbors are people who may be reluctant to seek out a faith community because their own experiences and ideas of religion. A pet ministry can offer a gentle entry point. Religiously unaffiliated persons may feel more comfortable participating in therapy dog training hosted by a church, where the community includes handlers, trainers, and their pets. At a time when it is difficult to build meaningful face-to-face connections, pet ministry can serve as a non-threatening way to share a more gracious, inclusive theology—one that acknowledges and honors the fullness of a family, including their beloved animals.

Another unmet need we continue to see is social isolation, which again was exacerbated by the COVID-19 pandemic. As people were required to keep their distance, many began to work remotely—and some still do. Children and teachers had to adapt to online education. On top of these adjustments, the shift also disrupted emotional health, physical health, and well-being by creating barriers that made it harder to form deep, lasting relationships.

Additionally, as people age, social isolation can become more profound. Health limitations, the death of friends, and fewer opportunities for connection can lead to loneliness, depression, and cognitive decline. In our experience, therapy dogs serving in rehab centers, retirement homes, and memory care facilities can help alleviate this isolation. Often, the presence of a dog brings back fond memories of a beloved pet. What's most powerful is the dog's non-anxious presence—it doesn't see the surgical scar, mobility aid, or a person's age. It simply shows up with warmth and affection.

Pet ministry can also help another, urgent social need: children's literacy. One out of every five U.S. adults is illiterate and more than half of adults have literacy skills below a sixth-grade level—an issue that costs the U.S. economy trillions of dollars.[7] One way pet ministry, particularly therapy dogs, can help overcome illiteracy and promote reading is through partnerships between faith groups, nonprofits, and local schools. Organizations like Pet Partners' "We Are All Ears" initiative or BARK Reading Therapy Dogs can help people of faith and their therapy animals to serve kids by listening to them practice in a safe, non-judgmental setting.

One of Betsy's dogs, Dottie, participated weekly in a third grade reading class, patiently listening to children as they read books aloud. That year, Dottie received more Christmas cards from the children at the school where she served than Betsy's own human family received!

Another urgent area of social need is mental health. According to the Kaiser Family Foundation, an overwhelming majority of Americans—nine out of ten—believe this country is experiencing a mental health crisis. In their 2022 survey, respondents ranked the opioid epidemic as one of the top concerns, with more than two-thirds identifying it as a crisis rather than simply a problem. Over half of those surveyed cited mental health struggles among children and teenagers as a crisis, and a similar number said the same about severe mental illness in adults. The lingering effects of the pandemic, and other threats such as systemic racism and gun violence, were also identified as contributing factors.[8]

Pew Research added to this conversation with a 2024 survey about teens, social media, and technology, highlighting the near-constant use of digital platforms by American youth. While some apps foster connection,

7. The National Literacy Institute, "Literacy Statistics 2024–2025," accessed May 29, 2025, https://www.thenationalliteracyinstitute.com/post/literacy-statistics-2024-2025-where-we-are-now.

8. Kaiser Family Foundation, "KFF/CNN Mental Health in America Survey Findings," October 5, 2022, https://www.kff.org/report-section/kff-cnn-mental-health-in-america-survey-findings/.

heavy use has the potential to limit face-to-face interactions, leaving users increasingly less engaged in real-world relationships.[9]

To respond to this multitude of needs, faith communities can incorporate trained therapy dogs in worship settings to greet attendees, as our congregation does, or recommend facilities where these trained and certified dogs or other therapy animals can offer comfort and reduce stress and anxiety. To prepare for more extreme and acute situations—like in the wake of a disaster or mass shooting—some individuals choose to become certified with a team such as NATIONAL Crisis Response Canines. This organization demands intensive preparation and specializes in the complex physical environments present in disaster areas and provides emotional support to people coping with trauma in the aftermath of a crisis. While highly selective, this represents another meaningful way faith communities can respond when emotional needs are urgent and unpredictable.

Social Polarization

For more than a decade the United States has become increasingly polarized—fueled by social media, disinformation, highly-charged political divisions, and contentious debates over topics like pandemic policy, gun violence, abortion, immigration, climate change, and civil rights. Public shaming, ridicule, and personal attacks have replaced dialogue. Normal discourse is strained at best, and is often volatile.

In 2016, amid this emerging environment, the dog food company Pedigree conducted a social experiment. They aired an ad that began with the narrator saying, "This election has brought out the worst in us. We sought to remind people what brings out the good." The commercial then shifts to follow a woman with a "lost" dog she claims to have found. She brings the dog to both Clinton and Trump rallies, clearly signaling

9. Pew Research Center, "Teens, Social Media, and Mental Health," April 22, 2025, https://www.pewresearch.org/internet/2025/04/22/teens-social-media-and-mental-health/.

support for the opposing candidate at each. The viewer watches as she asks strangers for help in finding the dog's owner. Despite political differences, attendees at both rallied respond with kindness. One man even responds, "I've been a dog lover forever. Dogs don't criticize."

That man's assessment has stuck with us when we think about the impact of pets. Pets soften our edges, they create an atmosphere of safety, break tension, and offer common ground. Pet ministry has the opportunity to do the same. When division has become the norm, churches can model unity, not by glossing over differences but by coming together around the one member of the family we all seem to accept and love: our pets. This can begin to bring us back together.

Some congregations may excel at offering recovery groups, Bible studies about difficult topics, traditional ministries for children, or visiting to older adults. These are all deeply valuable pursuits. Nevertheless, we believe that pet ministry offers a unique way to address broader social issues and respond to the particular unmet needs of people and communities today. Pet ministries can be as diverse and inclusive as the people who create them, shaped by the particular contexts and needs from which they emerge.

Pet ministry is a new way to care for a different group of people. For the two-thirds of Christians who claim that religious identity but do not actively belong to a church community, we wonder if they might join in if their pets were regularly acknowledged and welcomed? And if they do join in, if they feel welcomed and acknowledged alongside their pets, what might that mean for them? And what good might that do for all of us?

Discussion Questions

1. In what ways does a pet ministry respond to current social needs like loneliness, mental health challenges, and anxiety? How might this form of ministry be uniquely positioned to reach people who feel excluded or spiritually adrift?

2. What does it say about our theology and understanding of community when we welcome pets into our ministries and sacred spaces? How can this shift help us reimagine what it means to be inclusive, compassionate, and connected?
3. In recent years, the definition of family has shifted to more often include pets. How can churches expand their vision of "family ministry" to include the bond between humans and animals? What new possibilities does that open for intergenerational connection and pastoral care?
4. In an increasingly polarized and anxious world, what role could pets play in healing divisions and fostering trust within and beyond the church? How can a pet ministry become a space of common ground and gentle invitation?

RVANA

CHAPTER 16

Potential Pet Ministries

During COVID-19, *National Geographic*'s newsletter published an article as part of their daily update that asked the question, "Do we need our pets now more than they need us?" The author noted that almost half (43%) of people said they were playing with their dogs more during the nationwide shutdown. People also reported more engagement with all their pets, and many adopted new pets during this time.[1]

It's sometimes hard to believe how long ago our cross-species relationship with animals was first forged. In 1914, archaeologists in Germany discovered a fourteen-thousand-year-old burial site that is the earliest known example of humans and a dog being purposefully interred together.[2] We've been friends with animals for a very long time.

This deep bond we have with our pets is one that churches and other communities can and should acknowledge and respect. At the same time,

1. National Geographic, "Do We Need Pets More Now Than They Need Us?," *Animals Newsletter*, April 16, 2020, https://www.nationalgeographic.com/newsletters/animals/article/do-need-pets-more-now-than-they-need-us-april-16.
2. Franz Lidz, "This Ancient Dog Lived 14,000 Years Ago—and Was Loved," *National Geographic*, January 13, 2021, https://www.nationalgeographic.com/history/article/ancient-pet-puppy-oberkassel-stone-age-dog.

we must also remember that some people do not like dogs, cats, or other traditional pets, while others may extend their love and care toward a horse, rabbit, bird, or another, possibly more exotic animal. We also need to be mindful of allergies and other issues, including fear, that can create barriers for some, and determine the best ways to support all involved. What we all have in common is the reality that we live on the same planet, and our lives are deeply intertwined with all living beings. Pet ministry can be an opportunity to teach about animals and is one way we can affirm this connection and care for our fellow members of creation.

Faith communities and others devoted to service can find many ways to develop a pet ministry. Regardless of the direction a team chooses to take, any new ministry—especially one that may be considered outside the mainstream—should be explored with leaders. In churches, we would include clergy, laity, and other staff. The purpose of the ministry must also be carefully considered, clearly defined, and communicated thoroughly to the broader congregation.

In this chapter, our goal is to empower you and your community to consider whether a pet ministry is right for your congregation or group. We also want to help you think about how to select pet ministries that are right for your faith community, and what best practices to follow. Pet ministry is also an opportunity for interfaith collaboration and to work alongside non-religious people who share common goals of caring for the creation.

As we mentioned earlier, our first pet ministry began in 2007, with a Spirit-inspired nudge. Thankfully, we also received the immediate support of our congregation of about 150 people. Still, we understand that it can be challenging to start a new ministry or educate others about the purpose and vision of an uncommon ministry—especially one that might prompt shrieks of "We've never done that before!" That's why we recommend you start with a small group of interested individuals and build support gradually. It might be best to start small and work within an existing area of ministry. For example, a pet ministry can be a natural fit within the work of hospitality, outreach/service, worship, education, or even pastoral care.

Each pet ministry will be unique. Every context, faith community, and setting is different and will shape what type of pet ministry is possible and most appropriate. What works for one group may not work for another, and that's okay. Below are a few examples of pet ministry that a team might want to consider.

Care and Support for Pet People

Providing care and support for pet parents is similar to the ministry that we church folks call "pastoral care" or "congregational care." Pets are family members too, and as society increasingly recognizes them as such, it is important that we show care for people as they go through significant life transitions involving their animals. And this care can be extended to pet people both within and outside a faith community.

For example, families with pet companions have extra life events. As there is birth in families, so there is anticipation and joy with the arrival of a pet as a new family member. Sometimes new pets are babies; sometimes they are older, or even elderly. No matter what their age when an animal comes to their new home, we still celebrate the beginning of a new relationship. As mentioned, we have given new pet parents a pet prayer blanket as a sign of welcome.

We've sponsored a puppy socialization class and a webinar about how to take the best photos of pets—from reptiles to warm-blooded, furry mammals—while striving for the least amount of stress for everyone. We've offered access to pet education about the different kinds of animals living with us. We've distributed resources to help families care for their pets during holidays, especially when fireworks and loud noises can be distressing for animals. We've also shared information about toxic substances that should be avoided. We've invited therapy dogs to attend our denomination's annual conference gathering so that attendees can enjoy their meeting breaks by petting a dog. It's wonderful to watch children engage with the dogs, and it sends the signal that our church cares for animals, even as they show up for us.

Care might also take the shape of a public "pet fair" inviting local veterinarians to share about nutrition, spay/neuter, immunization, and microchipping. The event might also include rescue organizations, animal behaviorists, groomers, and vendors who can discuss the latest pet products.

Gayle and Betsy have waited with people whose pets were so ill that it became clear it was time to say goodbye. Simply being present to pet people during or after the death of a pet can provide comfort and validation of the importance of the relationship between person and beloved pet. After Betsy learned that a friend at her local gym lost her nineteen-year-old cat named Mister Sir, she delivered a pet prayer blanket. In return, Mister Sir's "mom" gave out beautiful cards that celebrated her cat's life and her gratitude for the support she'd received from so many during her loss.

One of our favorite ways to end the year is to send a Christmas card to all the people who we've come to know through our pet ministry. Looking at a year's worth of pet ministry photos reminds us how important this spiritual work really is and why we do it.

Therapy Dogs and Therapy Animals

Another type of pet ministry is offering therapy dog training classes and certification. Therapy dogs provide comfort, care, and encouragement in a wide range of settings, becoming a gentle yet powerful outreach in the broader community. They can be deployed to libraries, schools, hospitals, airports, and nursing care facilities—wherever people could use a little extra compassion.

Betsy suffers from C-PTSD (complex post-traumatic stress disorder), and her therapy dog, a golden retriever named Nilla, knew when she was hurting, distressed. or upset. If Betsy exhibited any sign of anxiety, Nilla would come sit with her and stare at her with concern until Betsy made eye contact with her and began to pet her. For Betsy, Nilla was a devoted healer.

While some people do have therapy animals other than dogs, most faith communities are not equipped to provide training for larger animals.

In our experience, we've found that dogs fit well in a ministry setting that can facilitate training and service. One reason is that dogs are natural healers. Studies have shown that most humans experience measurable health benefits from having a relationship with a dog (the same is true for cats and other pets). These people report lower blood pressure, slower heart rate, and elevated levels of serotonin and dopamine, which help to calm and relax us. Pet owners also tend to have lower cholesterol and triglyceride levels, and heart patients with pets often live longer.[3]

Another reason dogs fit well in a ministry of therapy animals is their deep love for people. Most dogs are xenophiles, meaning they tend to like everyone. In a time of increasing social division—politically, religiously, and culturally—dogs can be a unifying presence. We've observed people who disagree with each other in numerous ways come together through their shared love of dogs. And perhaps even more importantly, their dogs love them no matter what their opinions. This kind of gracious, unconditional love offers a model for us to follow. People can disagree, and still, we can love. Dogs do it instinctively.

Having promoted the ministry of therapy dogs within church settings, we also acknowledge a vital distinction: animals are not people. It's important to avoid projecting our own feelings or expectations onto their experience. While the bond between humans and animals is strong, people bear unique responsibilities in their role as animal caregivers. Scientists continue to remind us that all animals have their own perspective on the world and see it through their own lens. In a later chapter, we'll discuss how we can actively advocate for and respect other species more intentionally.

---

3. Erika Friedmann et al., "Animal Companions and One-Year Survival of Patients after Discharge from a Coronary Care Unit," *Public Health Reports* 97, no. 4 (July–August 1982): 376–81, https://pubmed.ncbi.nlm.nih.gov/12271103/.

Community Service Projects

Pet ministry can take the form of hands-on service projects. In this model, ministry teams can organize or support local events such as spay and neuter clinics, pet microchipping drives, pet adoption events in partnership with rescue groups, or pet food collection efforts for a local animal shelter or food pantry.

Some groups may also explore more in-depth work, such as helping create an emergency veterinary fund or forming partnerships with local vets to offer affordable vaccinations and physical exams. Both are ways to assist pet families who have limited resources.

Whatever focus a team chooses, projects should be defined by the needs of the community. A good starting point might include conducting a survey, collecting local data, and holding listening sessions with local animal welfare organizations to identify gaps in care and support.

Educational Programs

Educational programs are another avenue pet ministries can take. Hosting in-person workshops or online webinars with knowledgeable professionals can equip pet parents with valuable tools to better understand their animals and provide a better life for their pet. Some potential workshop topics include:

- Addressing pet behavior issues
- Dealing with separation anxiety
- How to select the best pet for one's household
- Basic pet first aid
- Answering questions about pet insurance
- Learning about local legal requirements, such as leash laws
- End-of-life care (both for the caregiver and the pet)
- When and how to make decisions about pet euthanasia
- How to plan a pet memorial

To illustrate the importance of practical education, consider this: recent studies have shown that women are more likely than men to injure themselves while walking their dog.[4] Although most of the injuries recorded were finger fractures and shoulder strains, more serious injuries to be aware of include traumatic brain injury. In response, a pet ministry could host a class on how to properly leash and walk a dog—for both the human's health and safety and the person's.

Pet Celebration Events

Faith communities also have the opportunity to celebrate people's relationships with their pets through special events. Pet ministries can host a celebration of the Feast of St. Francis of Assisi, an annual time to offer animal blessings in recognition of their sacred place in creation. Other meaningful observances include World Pet Memorial Day, a time to remember and honor pets who have passed away, as well as nationally recognized days of celebration, such as National Dog Day, which honors the bond between dogs and their humans. As we mentioned earlier, faith communities may publicize and join in celebrations with local businesses that welcome pets into their spaces for holidays like Mardi Gras, Halloween, and Valentine's Day.

Animal Advocacy

Advocating for the well-being of domestic animals—and animals more broadly—is another powerful way to support both pets and the people who love them. This advocacy can take many forms including:

- Promoting and supporting local, state, and federal laws around animal safety and animal welfare.

---

4. Harvard Health Publishing, "Women More Likely to Be Injured While Walking a Leashed Dog," *Harvard Health*, March 2023, https://www.health.harvard.edu/staying-healthy/women-more-likely-to-be-injured-while-walking-a-leashed-dog.

- Encouraging the passage of animal anti-cruelty legislation.
- Supporting the humane and ethical treatment of farm animals, livestock, and seeking alternatives to the use of laboratory animals in research.

A church and ministry committed to pet welfare and pet therapy can serve as an excellent host for events that raise awareness about these issues and others. Consider inviting experts and elected officials to speak about these issues and discuss them in a forum where diverse voices can be heard. These conversations can inspire action and build compassionate community engagement.

Discussion Questions

1. How does recognizing the deep emotional, physical, and spiritual bond between people and animals expand your understanding of what ministry can be? What would it mean for a church to take that bond seriously in both pastoral care and outreach?
2. What barriers—cultural, practical, or theological—do you think might exist in your community when it comes to launching a pet ministry? What would it look like to start small within an existing ministry to help build understanding and support? What ministries would work best for this project?
3. Pets create bridges across political, generational, and spiritual divides. How might a pet ministry become a tool for unity in a divided world?
4. This chapter outlines many ways a pet ministry could take shape. Which of these possibilities speaks most to your community's gifts, needs, and context? What's one small, practical step you or your group could take to explore this ministry further?

CHAPTER 17

How to Start a Pet Ministry

When people welcome a new pet into their home, most understand that there will be certain accommodations—changes in living space, daily routines, and financial costs. It also takes time to build mature and positive communication between the pet and its new family. Similarly, launching a new ministry or outreach within a faith community requires thoughtful preparation. Those involved will want additional information, education, and a clear sense of how they might serve with and on behalf of animals and their families. Starting a pet ministry begins with vision and planning because these are essential to guiding how the ministry develops and takes shape.

People interested in this work will need to prioritize what they can and cannot do based on their unique contexts. For example, a therapy dog ministry may encounter concerns about allergies, a fear of animals, concerns about cleanliness, or liability issues—especially if the group wants to host therapy dogs in a church building. Not every congregation will choose to hold training classes or invite animals onto their campus.

Therapy dog ministry in particular involves intensive preparation. Dogs and their handlers undergo extensive training, pass examinations, earn certifications, and receive ongoing education. These animals differ from emotional support animals for individuals, nor are they service dogs trained to assist individuals with specific mental or physical needs. Instead, therapy dogs are trained to bring comfort, share love, and provide joy to people in many settings. Their task is simple but profound: to love people. While incredibly meaningful, this form of ministry also requires a higher level of commitment and is more demanding than other types of pet ministry.

Initially, a team committed to launching a pet ministry must gather information about their local context—specifically, who might benefit most from their ministry and what areas of need are either urgent or realistic to support. Early on, a team might consider what initial endeavor would provide the greatest impact on the people and pets in the nearby community. For instance, would starting a pet food pantry within an existing food pantry be a meaningful first step?

Other important questions to consider include: What are the financial costs of a particular outreach? What would a basic budget look like? Who are potential partners within the local community? How can they help to provide financial support, volunteer support, or infrastructure? Partners might include nonprofits, veterinarians, pet behavior specialists, pet organizations, pet supply companies, local businesses, and mental health organizations—especially those who recognize the emotional and therapeutic benefits of human-animal interaction in helping to reduce stress and encourage mindfulness.

For those starting a pet ministry within a faith community, building a foundation of trust, education, and understanding with other ministry leaders is critical. Each congregation will differ in its structure and protocols, some may require a team to get formal permission or—at the very least—early buy-in from leadership to proceed. That's why we recommend first gathering facts and statistics, deciding on initial priorities, and identifying the type of pet ministry your team feels called to pursue.

Once that groundwork is laid, it is wise to approach a pastor or congregational leader who oversees the relevant ministry area—such as pastoral care, evangelism, outreach, advocacy, hospitality, or education. The team may need to prepare a presentation that provides other leaders with the purpose, goals, and benefits of the proposed ministry, supported by relevant facts and statistics. Gaining early support and a group commitment helps avoid problems and resistance that can occur if communication is lacking or if the initiative is a surprise.

In all settings, it's essential to keep the key leaders of the organization informed as the ministry or outreach develops. This includes regularly reporting progress to the appropriate people, celebrating milestones, and collaborating with communications staff within the church. There will likely be a need to prepare educational materials—both printed and digital—as well as design appropriate graphics or branding for the ministry.

The pet ministry team should establish clear timelines for launching the ministry, both internally (within the group) and externally (for the broader congregation). Teams also need to share details about what's involved with the ministry in order to recruit more volunteers or invite others who are interested in the ministry, including outside partners. As more people express interest and offer their skills and talents to help grow the project, leaders will want to maintain a database to track participation and support for future development.

Finally, the team will need to continually educate the congregation about the purpose of the ministry, including what it does and how it will impact both those in the pews and the wider community it seeks to serve. While creating a pet ministry will require planning and effort, there are clear rewards, both for those leading the ministry, those supporting it within the congregation, and those who are served by it in the wider world.

Discussion Questions

1. What needs—both inside and outside the congregation—might a pet ministry be uniquely qualified to address in your community? Who in your community will benefit from this outreach, and what kind of care could you offer?

2. What types of pet ministry feel most aligned with your church's gifts, space, and people? Pastoral care? Education? Community service? Therapy dog work? What would be the easiest place to start, and what might require more planning and preparation?
3. What challenges or concerns can you see arising when introducing animals into a ministry context? How can your group respectfully prepare for and address these concerns with transparency and care?
4. How can you or your team begin building support for this idea within the church's leadership and broader community? What steps would be helpful in gaining early buy-in?

CHAPTER 18

Caring for Families and Their Pets

A common ministry in faith communities is congregational care, which often encompasses spiritual, emotional, and mental well-being. While informal communities also look out for one another in times of change, stress, illness, and loss, this type of organized care is designed to pay specific attention to the needs of the people within the church, including both times of joy and seasons of pain and hardship. A pet ministry can do the same and amplify the work of congregational care by paying attention to the people who have pets and the pets themselves who are part of those families.

As mentioned earlier, teams can send a card or pet prayer blanket to a family to express joy and welcome at a new pet's arrival. In our community, we also have a sewing team that creates specially sized fleece blankets for pets, choosing a particular fabric so that pets will not get their claws caught in these "pet prayer blankets." For those groups who are not religiously affiliated, they might prefer to use the term "pet welcome blanket."

Teams may provide care through pet adoption support. In one family, a couple struggling with the husband's ALS diagnosis lost their longtime terrier. The dog was a balm for both the wife, Rebecca, who had provided constant, loving care for her husband, Bernie, who was at home, and whose only mobility was using his eyes to type on a computer.

In the wake of their loss, Rebecca contacted our pet coordinator to assist in finding a new companion dog. While the immediate cause of her grief was the loss of their pet, she was also grieving her husband's progressive illness and had been for over a decade. Rebecca was overwhelmed at the prospect of looking for a new dog, but she also wanted the comfort and companionship that she knew a new dog would bring to their family. Our pet coordinator helped her search and locate a new dog, offering yet another way that a pet ministry or pet team can provide a unique form of pastoral care. The caring support was taken to another level when the coordinator and the pastor presented a pet prayer blanket to Rebecca and Bernie at their home and offered a prayer of thanksgiving for the pet's welcome.

Additionally, pet ministries can provide emotional support when an animal becomes sick or dies. We carefully monitor our social media and encourage our congregation to stay attentive for these painful seasons in people's lives. In our church, when members hear about the death of a pet—like when a member of our community became aware of his former co-worker's loss—they contact the pet ministry, retrieve a blanket, and deliver it to the bereaved family. The pet coordinator keeps a record of all the distributed blankets to help us keep track of the scope of the ministry and ensure that we offer follow-up care. Grief is a difficult process, and we are mindful of the ways we can continue to support the family of the deceased pet over time.

Ministries can also extend care to one another's pets in distinct and emotionally sensitive circumstances. One church held a memorial service for a young woman who had died of a serious illness. She had two elderly dogs, and during the service, those pets needed someone present in the home to care for them, especially since the disruption to their routine and the absence of their owner were causing so much stress. The family of the woman was at the memorial service and was unable to watch over them.

In response, members of that community who were trained to care for dogs volunteered to take shifts during the day of the memorial service. One of the dogs sat beside the young woman's bed, gazing out the window as if he were patiently waiting for her return. The dogs, who were both blind and hard of hearing, benefited greatly from the calm presence of those volunteers. Their attentive care made a real difference for the pets and brought comfort to the family. Spending significant time at the family's home also reminded those involved that simply being present was a gift to the pets, the family, and the ones staying with the pets. Sometimes the mere act of presence—showing up and showing compassion—is the greatest gift we can give.

In our experience, the hardest season in which to care for a family and their beloved pet is when they have to say goodbye to the animal who is truly a member of their family. When walking through these hard times, a member of a pet ministry or care team might offer to accompany a person or even a family to the veterinarian if the pet needs to be euthanized. This support can be especially meaningful if the pet has become suddenly ill or when it is clear that the pet will not survive after receiving treatment. In these situations, the sense of loss can be profound, especially for single pet parents.

Public expressions of grief for beloved pets are widely seen and supported on social media. These platforms have helped society better understand and validate the emotional weight of losing a pet. Kirk Herbstreit, a well-known ESPN and Amazon Prime sports analyst, lost his dog Ben—who had traveled with him to many of the college football games that Herbstreit worked. When Ben passed away after battling cancer, Herbstreit expressed his thanks for the outpouring of love, support, and care from fans on social media. Tributes to Ben followed, reminding us of the ways pets are woven into the fabric of our lives—our work, our play, and even our national pastimes.

There are numerous ways to care for people as they move through the process of grief that follows the loss of a pet. As we shared earlier, pet prayer blankets often become cherished keepsakes and can even be lovingly used to say goodbye. A woman we know named Marie, requested a blanket for her sick, twenty-two-year-old cat. Unfortunately, the day after sending the request, the pet had died. Although Marie didn't receive the blanket before the pet passed away, she nevertheless accepted the special blanket, using it to wrap her beloved companion before burying her. The blanket became a burial shroud, a final act of love and remembrance to celebrate and honor the life of a beloved cat.

We gave a dog trainer a pet prayer blanket to grieve her pet. Red was a beautiful championship German shepherd, just two qualifying runs away from earning a Barn Hunt Championship when she became ill. Pam, her handler and trainer, rushed Red to the emergency veterinary hospital. Gayle, representing the pet ministry, met Pam at the emergency room and gave her a prayer blanket. The emergency team allowed the blanket to be placed over Red as she fought for her life for several hours. Sadly, Red succumbed to her illness and passed away later that night.

Pam slept with the prayer blanket for a week, then transformed it into a heart-shaped pillow made from the same fabric, memorializing her deep love for Red. The pillow now holds a special place in her home, allowing Pam to always have Red near her.

In the aftermath of a pet's death, some pet ministry teams extend their care by helping plan memorial services, offering a presence at the service, and providing grief support through structured curriculum designed specifically for the loss of a pet.

Kay's beloved golden retriever, Molly, was a certified therapy dog who made regular visits throughout the community, including to nursing care facilities, rehab units, and public libraries. Molly visited people in these settings weekly and her presence was a source of comfort and joy to everyone. When she died, it wasn't just Kay who grieved, but an entire group of people who mourned the loss of Molly. Even one of the doctors at the rehab unit was moved to tears having been so affected by the emotional bond he formed with Molly.

In response to Kay's loss, our pet ministry coordinator asked Kay if she would like to hold a memorial service for Molly. Kay believed that

Molly—who had always been a loving and social dog—would have wanted her friends nearby. With assistance from the pet ministry coordinator, who had previously helped with Molly's therapy certification, they invited three representatives from each of the communities Molly had visited to speak at her service, which was held at a nearby Episcopal church.

The deacon—who also had a therapy dog—and the pet ministry coordinator co-wrote the liturgy for the service and presided over the memorial. The sanctuary was filled with people who had known and loved Molly and were grieving her loss. A memory table invited attendees to bring reminders of Molly. One librarian from a children's library brought drawings of Molly created by kids who had read to her during her participation in the Tail Waggin' Tutors program. The table was filled with delightful illustrations of this beloved dog, made by people whose lives she had touched.

Following the service, mourners gathered for a reception with refreshments. Many of Molly's friends stayed for a long time, sharing stories about her and expressing their grief. Molly had brought people together in life—and in her passing, she continued to foster community and care.

The most difficult time for pet parents usually is when their pets are ill or when they suffer the loss of a beloved pet. We've heard people apologize for their grief, but grief is not measured by who we love, but the depth of love, and many pet people consider their pets to be family. For some, their pet is the only family or the closest family. Pet ministries can provide help for families during a pet's illness, being present for euthanasia, anointing the body with oil, prayer, the grief process, how to write a pet obituary, and even guide them in a ritual such as a memorial that brings community support and care.

Discussion Questions

1. How do our relationships with pets mirror the deep emotional, spiritual, and familial connections we often share with one another? How might a pet ministry honor and support these bonds?
2. What are some practical ways your congregation could extend pastoral care to people at different stages of life with a pet—such as adoption, illness, or death? What might feel comforting or sacred in those moments?
3. This chapter highlights how grief over a pet can be just as real and profound as grief over a human loved one. Why do you think this kind of loss is sometimes overlooked, and how might the church help validate and tend to that grief?
4. What gifts, skills, or callings do you see in yourself or others that support this type of ministry for pets and their caregivers? Where could you start to apply these gifts and skills?

CHAPTER 19

Therapy Animals: Pets in Ministry with People

Ernie was a Great Pyrenees rescue—a gigantic, fluffy white dog with a soulful expression and a gentle personality. Ernie became a therapy dog, and his handler, Leslie, got involved with Court Appointed Special Advocates (CASA), a national association that provides trained court-appointed advocates to support neglected or abused children and help place them in safer, healthier, and permanent homes.

One holiday season, Leslie and Ernie went to a CASA open house attended by social workers, judges, and clerks. There was a special guest appearance by Santa! Ernie was a big hit. He and Leslie were soon invited to regularly attend family meetings to help ease the children's anxiety. Several judges told Leslie they wanted Ernie to be a regular presence in their courtrooms, particularly for children waiting in a witness holding room before testifying in a public courtroom.

During the event, children currently in foster care were welcomed in to meet Santa. A four-year-old boy arrived with his grandfather and his CASA advocate. The boy was so happy when he saw Ernie that he paid little attention to Santa. The boy smiled and laughed and hugged the friendly dog. Then, the child leaned in close to Ernie's ear and whispered, "It's okay. It's okay. It's okay."

The advocate couldn't hear what the boy was saying and asked Leslie. Leslie repeated the word. The advocate was stunned. She explained that the boy was autistic and non-verbal. He did not speak to anyone—until now. He spoke to Ernie with ease, calmly and clearly.

We're proud to say that our church's therapy dog ministry trained Ernie.

Certified Therapy Animals

As many of our stories highlight, dogs are the most common therapy animals. However, other types of animals also work with their handlers to provide meaningful visits and healing experiences for those in need of them. Pet Partners, a therapy animal certifying organization, equips and supports volunteer therapy animals to "help improve the physical, social, and emotional lives of both the people and animals involved."[1] They promote interactions with a variety of animals and currently register nine types of animals for therapy visits: dogs, cats, horses, rabbits, guinea pigs, rats, birds, miniature pigs, and llamas/alpacas.

This diverse and lengthy list of eligible animals is a reminder that pet ministry can take many forms and look different in different contexts. A rural congregation, for example, may be able to accommodate larger animals and bring people to them—think horses, donkeys—for therapeutic interactions. Some certifying organizations even offer mindfulness experiences to pet-friendly employers, sending therapy animal teams to participate in corporate conventions, industry expos, or employee wellness events through specific partnerships.

Individuals who wish to become therapy animal handlers must qualify with an official certifying organization. They also must adhere to the group's policies and procedures. The certification process is often quite stringent and includes obedience and behavioral testing, rule compliance,

1. "About Us," *Pet Partners*, accessed May 29, 2025, https://petpartners.org/about/.

and official licensing. Some organizations also require a criminal background check for people over eighteen years of age.

Because of the wide array of possible ministries involving different pets—and the almost limitless range of geographical contexts (rural, urban, suburban, and so forth)—along with varying levels of socio-economic diversity, your faith community or group can serve as an important bridge. You can help translate and communicate the necessary details required to train and support therapy animals. It is especially important to educate pet families about what will be expected of them to participate in this kind of service.

Our pet ministry experience has primarily involved therapy dogs, but the steps we've followed in developing a therapy dog ministry can also help guide others who want to work with different animals as therapy pets. As part of a faith community, we understand that healing and wholeness can come in many forms—through modern medicine, through loving touch and prayer as modeled by Jesus, and through companionship during times of trauma, anxiety, sickness, grief, or dislocation. This kind of healing is needed daily, whether in rehab facilities where people are recovering from surgery, or when a child or older adult feels lonely and isolated.

Some animals, though not officially certified, still serve informally in community spaces—brought by responsible caregivers who recognize their pet's calming presence. One such example is a pet pig named Odin, who became a beloved visitor at a long-term care facility in Olathe, Kansas. After a maintenance worker, Brett Martin, asked the facility administrator for permission to bring his one-year-old companion to work, Odin quickly became part of the daily rhythm. Fully vaccinated, leash and litter-box-trained, Odin was granted permission by the director even though he wasn't certified as a therapy animal.

For many residents—especially those who grew up on farms—his presence felt familiar and provided a source of comfort. "He's an instant stress reliever for everyone who interacts with him," Martin said about his friend and pet pig. One memory care resident, a retired farmer living with Alzheimer's disease, gets visibly excited every time Odin visits. The residents enjoy petting him and feeding him snacks, and he enjoys the attention of the residents and staff, along with several cats and dogs who occasionally come to work with their pet parents. Odin could, of course, be certified as a therapy animal, but even without the official title, his impact is clearly profound.[2]

Pet therapy animals are particularly valuable when people experience disasters, which have been happening more frequently due to climate change. As a result, public officials and emergency management coordinators are increasingly recognizing the importance of providing shelters that accommodate both people and their pets during evacuations. Many people are unwilling to leave their pets behind in harm's way. In Florida, where hurricanes are a regular threat, government officials attributed the high rate of evacuation during Hurricane Milton to the availability of safe shelters for people with pets. Additionally, shelter animals were transported to out-of-state facilities to ensure continued care.

Sadly, another growing area of service for therapy animals comes in response to mass shootings. After the tragedy at Sandy Hook Elementary, as well as similar incidents, therapy dogs specially trained to deal with trauma were brought in to comfort children. With the help of these dogs, children and teenagers were able to open up and begin to share about their experiences, speaking openly with the dogs in a way that they were unable to do with family members or other adults. This kind of healing is made possible by a dog's innate ability to listen without judgment while demonstrating unconditional love.

During the upheaval of the COVID-19 pandemic, even when handlers and therapy dogs were unable to enter facilities due to restrictions, they still found ways to provide comfort. Some therapy teams visited retirement centers and stood outside windows, offering cheerful greetings from a distance and brightening the residents' days.

---

2. Cathy Free, "Pet Pig Visits Senior Home Each Day: 'They're Very Social Animals,'" *Washington Post*, November 23, 2024. https://www.washingtonpost.com/lifestyle/2024/11/23/miniature-pig-senior-center-kansas/.

Steps to Developing a Therapy Dog Ministry

The primary hurdle when starting a pet ministry—especially one focused on training and using therapy dogs—is helping people understand what therapy dogs actually do. Many individuals and institutions, whether churches or service organizations, are unfamiliar with the role, training, and certification process required for therapy dogs. Most have never seen a working model like this in action. Education is critical.

We've offered therapy dog training in four different congregational settings. Whether your team is operating within a small or large church, it's essential for the team to help the community understand the level of commitment involved in launching a therapy dog ministry. Once there's a shared understanding in the community, a team of committed and diverse volunteers and ministry leaders can begin to plan the specifics.

There are two main paths for incorporating therapy dogs. The first is that a team can choose to invite dogs from the community that are already certified through a recognized organization. In this model, the responsibility for training, certification, and administrative details fall on the pet handler. Some reputable certifying organizations include:

- Alliance of Therapy Dogs
- Bright and Beautiful Therapy Dogs
- Love on a Leash
- Pet Partners

The second option is to start your own training program within your congregation, though this will require additional structure and follow-through. The first step is to identify a skilled and reliable dog trainer—someone who not only loves dogs but also has experience working with them, connects well with people, and possesses plenty of patience. The trainer may be the first point of contact many people have with your pet ministry, so it's essential that they represent your values well. In faith-based contexts, the therapy dogs may also become the public face of your church in the community.

Ideally, the trainer is a professional or behavioral specialist and is familiar with the standards of therapy dog certifying organizations. If a certified professional isn't available locally, you can still find a qualified trainer by checking the websites of organizations like the American Kennel Club or the Association of Professional Dog Trainers. Both organizations provide a search database and offer guidelines, including age requirements for handlers.

The advantage of a church or faith-based community offering therapy dog classes is that it allows people unfamiliar with your church to become acquainted with your people, your campus, and to find a place of welcome in a communal setting. A strong sense of hospitality is important, and it's helpful for a pastor, as well as other team members, to welcome new people from outside the congregation when they attend classes in your church building.

Keep in mind that some attendees may know very little about Christianity, and some may even have negative perceptions of Christians. That's why your team should consistently strive to embody a spirit of generosity and kindness, showing care through warm words and inclusive actions. It's important to avoid any behavior that could be seen as exclusionary or judgmental.

The expectation for everyone—church members and guests alike—is that they are participating in a class that will build supportive relationships with other handlers and their dogs. Later, those who complete certification may be invited to participate in ministry activities, such as greeting at worship services, or being present at Vacation Bible School and other events.

When planning events that involve dogs, particularly those open to children or the wider community, it's important for pet ministries to communicate clearly in advance that therapy dogs will be present. Use these moments as teaching opportunities to help children learn good manners and how to treat animals with respect and care. Even though therapy dogs are trained and carefully certified, we all share responsibility for teaching others how to engage with our therapy dogs—and all animals—in a healthy way.

For all these reasons, hosting therapy dog classes at your church can be a real advantage. Ideally, the best space on a church campus would be a large gym, gathering hall, local community center, or a flat area outside, covered, if possible, for inclement weather. The key is having enough room for all the dogs and handlers to spread out comfortably, along with providing easy access to bathrooms.

If your team goes this route and is working to locate a dog trainer, remember that it's also important to consider the financial equation. The ideal scenario would be finding a trainer who will donate their time, allowing the ministry to offer the class at no cost to participants. In this situation, the only expense for participants would be the final certification exam and registering with the certifying organization.

In the more likely scenario that a trainer cannot donate their time, the team should seek funding from their faith community to cover the cost of at least the first class. In our experience, once people experience therapy dog training and the joy it brings, many are moved to donate. Over time, this generosity can help the ministry become financially self-sustaining.

As for the class format, we've found the most effective model includes a mandatory orientation session with handlers, followed by seven weeks of one-hour of classes. That initial meeting is crucial and should stress the importance and expectations around the commitment required and carefully explain the purpose of a therapy dog, as opposed to other sorts of dogs, such as emotional support dogs or service dogs. Additionally, the class leader should explain that the explicit goal of the training process is to regularly visit others alongside their certified dog. Furthermore, this orientation should introduce and demonstrate the type of dog training equipment that will be needed for training. Once the dogs are trained and certified, the handlers may choose the settings and types of service that best match their dog's temperament and their own interests.

One dog, Brandy, regularly visits special needs classes at a local high school. During her first visit, the teacher invited Brandy's handler to let the dog explore the classroom freely. On a later visit, Brandy connected with a teenage boy with facial differences that included a lack of facial muscle control. Brandy was drawn to the young man, and she quietly sat down beside him, patiently waiting to be petted. The student looked at the handler and said, "I can't smile, but I'm smiling!" Schools are a great place for handlers and their dogs to serve.

One of the most rewarding pet ministries a church or other group can offer is therapy dog training and deployment of the handlers and their animals for service to others. Of all the pet ministries, this one requires the most planning, organization, administration, and hands-on work. That's why we've included detailed instructions in our Sources and Resources section at the back of this book to help you determine whether or not this fulfilling and beneficial ministry is for your group.

Discussion Questions

1. What do you find most compelling or surprising about the ways therapy animals bring healing, connection, and comfort to people in need—from courtrooms to memory care facilities to schools? How might this affect the way your ministry looks outside the walls of a church?
2. What challenges or hesitations might your faith community need to overcome in order to embrace a therapy animal ministry?
3. The story of Ernie shows how a therapy animal can create space for communication, healing, and even speech where none existed before. What does that say about the spiritual and emotional power of nonverbal presence? How do we, as people of faith, honor that kind of quiet ministry?
4. What excites you or energizes you about taking the next step toward creating or becoming involved in a pet ministry?

CHAPTER 20

Community Service Projects to Benefit Animals

When considering service projects for people with pets and pets themselves, there are many ways to serve. To begin, we encourage you to take time to get to know your community—including veterinarians, rescue organizations, shelters, and pet behaviorists. All of these professionals offer a range of services and educational information that may inform the kinds of outreach or service your pet ministry prioritizes.

One year, our congregation partnered with an urgent care veterinary clinic to observe the Feast of St. Francis of Assisi. Many churches hold a Blessing of the Animals in early October near this day. Along with the blessing, our church invited the vet clinic to provide low-cost microchipping. This quick and painless procedure works similarly to a vaccine; the chip is injected under the skin of the pet and contains a unique ID number. That number is entered into a database along with the contact information of the pet's family. A scanner can read the chip, so if the animal is lost, its owner can be located. The chip is particularly useful when a name tag is lost or a pet has no other form of identification.

This event offered a valuable service to our church community and to our neighbors who might not otherwise be able to afford this form of pet identification. Those who attended with their pets received a blessing and had the opportunity to meet the pastor and other members of the congregation. It was a positive and enriching experience for the veterinary staff as well, allowing them to meet others and serve in a joyful setting rather than their usual high-stress emergency care environment. Both our congregation and the clinic staff were able to connect with the community in a different, life-affirming way.

Another way to serve veterinarians is by recognizing that clinics, especially emergency clinics, may be understaffed and in need of volunteers to provide non-medical support. Many clinics provide emergency funds for people whose pets become seriously ill and require costly tests, procedures, or surgeries. Often, people find themselves at an emergency clinic because they were unable to pay for preventive care. As a result, the cost of emergency services may be nearly catastrophic. Your ministry might consider partnering with these clinics by raising funds to help cover medical costs that people cannot afford. Your pet ministry could host a fundraiser specifically to benefit an emergency veterinarian fund.

Another way to serve is by connecting with local animal shelters. Most communities have stray animals or pets that have been surrendered to a shelter. Pet ministries may choose to focus on this pressing issue by working with local shelters or nonprofit organizations involved in pet rescue and adoption. Take time to learn about the various rescue organizations in your area and explore potential partnerships. Most cities and counties operate animal shelters that are constantly in need of support—whether through donations of blankets, food, supplies, or volunteer time. It's also important to acknowledge that not all shelters adopt out every pet, and sadly, many animals are still euthanized every day. Consider how your team might support the staff and volunteers who carry the emotional burden of that difficult work.

Your team may want to develop an ongoing relationship with a specific rescue organization and organize a signature event—either by hosting an on-site adoption day where several rescue groups bring animals to your church campus, or by holding a benefit to raise money for rescue efforts.

Some congregations prefer to sponsor an existing nonprofit event through a financial gift. A local rescue we've partnered with holds several annual fundraisers, and our church has regularly contributed at a sponsorship level. This support earns us a spot on signage, banners, t-shirts, and other event media while also supporting an organization whose mission aligns with our own.

In our hometown, one rescue organization puts on a fashion show called "Paws on the Runway." Sponsoring this kind of event is a meaningful way for a pet ministry to publicly demonstrate its dedication to the care of domestic animals. When people see that a religious group not only cares about animals but also actively gives its time and resources, it creates opportunities for connection. Those with the same passion for animal welfare may be drawn to a community that aligns with their values in this way.

Another option for service would be the creation of a pet pantry. Just like small food pantries and Little Free Libraries that spring up on the sidewalk, a team might consider founding a Little Free Pet Pantry. These mini pantries, designed specifically for pets, have been popping up in various communities. The idea is simple: provide a small, accessible space for people to donate pet-related items and to take what they need in turn. Donations may include pet food, leashes, collars, flea and tick prevention products, chew toys, grooming tools, or any other supplies needed to care for a pet. Projects like this can be organized and maintained by neighborhoods or groups of volunteers who commit to work together to assist in maintaining supplies and donations.

Another meaningful way to serve is by providing medical care for animals in underserved areas. We learned about the nonprofit Christian Veterinary Mission (CVM) through Drs. Jeanie and Jon Kendall, both veterinarians. The mission of CVM is "to challenge, empower, and facilitate veterinary professionals to serve others by living out their Christian faith."[1] The organization was founded after a woman at a bible study, living

1. Christian Veterinary Mission, "Core Organizational Documents," last modified April 22, 2024, https://cvm.org/Files/PDFs/CVM%20Core%20Organizational%20Documents%204-22-24.pdf.

in an under-developed country, expressed her community's greatest need: to have someone come and teach them veterinary skills so that residents could do the work for themselves. That conversation led to the formation of CVM and its mission to help poor farmers by offering needed expertise in the responsible care and breeding of animals.

On one of these trips, Jon Kendall met an eight-year-old boy named Jonathan in a remote village in Belize. Jon was going from house to house treating animals and quickly connected with the boy even though they didn't speak the same language. They shared a first name, a favorite color—orange—and a deep love for animals. Jonathan had a beloved pet dog. Jon and the visiting vets were able to vaccinate his dog for rabies, deworm her, and apply long-lasting flea and tick prevention. While the treatment had health benefits, it also offered something more personal: a deep recognition of Jonathan's bond with his dog.

Although CVM is an explicitly Christian organization, its work reflects a universal truth: caring for vulnerable people and their animals helps build stronger, healthier communities. And healthier communities are something the whole world needs.

Discussion Questions

1. How can our congregation identify and respond to the specific pet-related needs in our local community? What partnerships with vets, shelters or rescue groups might be especially meaningful for us to explore?
2. What are the spiritual and relational benefits of combining traditional church events (like the Blessing of the Animals) with practical services (like microchipping or adoption days)? How might these events reshape the way the church is viewed in the community?
3. In what ways could a Little Free Pet Pantry or emergency vet fund reflect our values of compassion, hospitality, and justice? What

challenges might we face in starting one of these initiatives and how could we overcome them?

4. How does caring for animals—especially in underserved communities—help us live out our calling to love our neighbors and serve the vulnerable? What other ways can respond to that calling through pet ministry?

CHAPTER 21

Education, Events, and Advocating for Animals

In the 1987 film *Raising Arizona*, an ex-con and an ex-cop marry, only to learn they cannot have children. After stealing a baby from a family with quintuplets, the "new dad" jumps in his getaway car and hands the baby off to the "new mom." He then tosses a book onto the car seat, saying, "Here's the instructions." The book is a copy of *Dr. Spock's Baby and Child Care.*

This exaggerated scene resonates with audiences because all parents need help, and that begins well before the baby arrives. At minimum, most parents read a few books or attend parenting classes. Many do much more. Yet the same is not necessarily true for pet parents. Many do not consider how much change a new family member will bring—particularly one who may have already developed coping mechanisms while living in dysfunctional settings like puppy mills or abusive and neglectful homes. Potential adoptive families may not have thought through issues like living space, exercise needs, financial responsibilities, potty training, grooming, or a pet's unique personality and existing habits.

That's one reason why pet education classes can be such a valuable support for pet families. They can improve both the adoption experience and, most importantly, the long-term success of keeping a pet. We encourage faith communities and other groups to offer classes on a wide range of topics—from how to choose a suitable pet to how to deal with behavioral problems or understanding how animals interpret human behavior. Our responses can either escalate stress in an animal or calm it. These classes can be held in person with pets or offered virtually through webinars or over Zoom.

Community events offer meaningful ways to work on behalf of animals and strengthen the bond between people and their pets. One event we host annually is a holiday worship service known as "Blue Christmas." This service recognizes the reality that many people struggle with depression, loss, and anxiety during the "festive" season. There's no need to pretend everything is joyful when life can be challenging. Instead, we intentionally create space to recognize change, the feeling of grief, and mental health struggles. We offer ways to be present with people who are hurting. After the service, all participants are invited to stay for cocoa and cookies, and therapy dogs are present to offer companionship, comfort, and a healing presence for those who want it.

Our event for World Pet Memorial Day (discussed in Chapter 16) which we co-sponsored with a local urgent care veterinary clinic was important for pet families. Through the people who attended, we learned about the depth of their grief, particularly because so many were not members of our church. Few faith communities acknowledge pets as a family members, but we believe this reluctance represents a missed opportunity to create a welcoming space for those experiencing real and profound grief.

We can also support animals through acts of advocacy, whether by voicing public support for certain policy positions or promoting changes that can improve animal health and welfare. Some individuals, within their religious traditions practice what's known as a *welfarist approach* when talking about issues related to companion or housed animals—they seek to ensure the best possible conditions for animals, whether they are pets, livestock, or animals in research labs.

While a ministry or small group may be united by a shared love of animals, members will inevitably hold different views on various local and national issues. Some will want to work toward improving conditions, while others pursue the goal of abolition—seeking to eliminate the use of animals in farming, captivity, or experimentation altogether.

Faith-based advocacy also isn't limited to just a single tradition. There are interfaith groups actively working for animal welfare. The Interfaith Vegan Coalition, for example, offers "religion-specific advocacy kits" as well as downloadable resources. Another example is the UK-based Animal Interfaith Alliance, an umbrella organization that includes Anglican, Buddhist, Catholic, Hindu, Jain, Jewish, Quaker, and Unitarian groups, as well as Animals in Islam.[1]

Animal rescue work encompasses not only shelter animals like dogs and cats, but also extends to larger animals—such as donkeys—often cared for in sanctuaries. Advocacy efforts in this realm can include promoting humane treatment, campaigning against the use of animals in certain products (some beauty items, for example, include ingredients made from donkey hides), opposing animal testing, and working for wildlife conservation.

Marcia McFee is an educator about Christian worship and liturgy. Marcia also incorporates examples of Jesus' ministry of care, justice, and compassion for the least of these, including our animal friends. Marcia's interest in donkey rescue was sparked during a trip to Devon, England, where she began researching donkeys—animals that appear frequently in biblical stories. Donkeys are often in need of rescue for many reasons: they have long life spans (typically twenty-seven to forty years) and are often the target of abuse and abandonment, while suffering from poor living conditions and severe neglect.

---

1. Sarah A. Bowen, *Sacred Sendoffs: An Animal Chaplain's Advice for Surviving Animal Loss, Making Life Meaningful, & Healing the Planet* (Minneapolis: Broadleaf Books, 2022), 150–51.

Near her home in Kansas City, Missouri, Marcia visited Zen Donkey Farm and Experience, a rescue haven created by Kate Barker Sternberg. The sanctuary's mission is to house and rehabilitate one hundred donkeys in need of a new life. To help younger Christians and others better understand these animals—especially around Advent and Christmas—Marcia produced educational videos that highlight how donkeys model traits we could all learn from: they are helpers, protectors, listeners, lovers, givers, and comforters.

In her educational videos, Marcia shares how the donkey sanctuary partners with nearby Children's Mercy Hospital, offering healing connections for children who, like the rescued donkeys, need extra love and care. When we spoke with Marcia, she emphasized the importance of advocacy and the need to teach others about what animals need from us. For instance, the common belief that donkeys are stubborn is a myth. In reality, donkeys are highly perceptive and sense danger in situations where humans don't. As a result, they may resist when in unsafe situations, protecting both themselves and us in the process. Lessons like this teach us that we are all part of the same creation, and we humans still have a lot to learn from our fellow creatures.

While sanctuaries for animals such as donkeys and elephants are needed, another animal organization that pet ministries can partner with are zoos. As we mentioned earlier, some who work on animal welfare and animal rights are not supportive of zoos, and there are many "zoos" who do not follow the guidelines or strict accreditation process of the AZA. Most AZA zoos are nonprofits or public institutions that promote conservation, education, science, and recreation.

While we've already expressed our support for AZA-accredited zoos, we understand that some people object to keeping any type of wild animals in enclosures, no matter how thoughtfully designed those spaces may be. The truth is that our species has a poor track record of caring for both wildlife and domestic animals—especially when it comes to how we care for the natural habitat on which animals depend. Because of our continued intrusion into animal ecosystems, we hold out hope that animal welfare efforts, conservation initiatives, educational programs, and strategies like the Species Survival Plan can help provide long-term support for wildlife and even support reintroduction efforts in the future. We also know that zoos support many employees who care about animals, and they need volunteers. Gayle's husband, Paul, has been a docent for our Little Rock AZA Zoo for decades, working with birds of prey.

We agree with Tripp York, who spent three years volunteering at the Virginia Zoo, when he writes, "Nonintervention is impossible. We intervene constantly–even when we are unaware of it. . . . The question is not whether we are going to intervene; the question is how we are going to intervene."[2]

Advocacy can also be a full-time vocation. Betsy's friend and colleague, Rev. Dr. Beth Cooper, who grew up on a farm, is an Animal Chaplain, animal advocate, Equine Assisted Learning Facilitator, and an ordained elder in the United Methodist Church. Her passion and ministry has always included work with animals.

One of Beth's emphases is palliative care. She visited a woman with dementia twice weekly with her four-pound dog Joey, an animal who was rescued and had an uncommon ability to provide comfort to those in transitions of life. Beth found out that when they weren't there, the patient would ask for Joey and talk about Joey, so Beth left a canvas picture of Joey in the patient's room. The patient never remembered Beth's name but never forgot Joey's. Joey helped the woman through a time of discomfort and anxiety. When the patient passed, her family put the picture of Joey on their wall at home, so their loved one could always see Joey, a little dog with a big heart.

Animal chaplaincy may be an unknown field of ministry, but it's an emerging area that has arisen out of a real need for spiritual and emotional care for animals and the humans who love them. Animal chaplains can

2. Sarah A. Bowen, *Sacred Sendoffs: An Animal Chaplain's Advice for Surviving Animal Loss, Making Life Meaningful, & Healing the Planet* (Minneapolis: Broadleaf Books, 2022), 150–51.

often provide end-of-life care and rituals, offer a theological understanding of our connection to creation, foster stronger emotional resilience, and support people dealing with compassion fatigue, especially those working in shelters, rescues, and veterinary care. Animal chaplains are uniquely suited to healing ministry, and they can provide a bridge between pet families, pets, and clinics, shelters, or anywhere animals are.[3]

Our work with and on behalf of animals—and the people who love them—is sometimes difficult and challenging, but more often, it's deeply beautiful. When someone calls us and asks if they can deliver a pet prayer blanket to a grieving person who has just lost their beloved companion, it's a powerful reminder that pet ministry educates people about the importance of animal companions. Events with our pets can also help us express our deeper emotions and remind us how much they give humans. We believe it is also important for us to advocate for all creatures, great and small, and to recognize it is a spiritual work.

Discussion Questions

1. In what ways can churches better support individuals and families navigating the emotional and spiritual challenges of pet adoption, care, and loss?
2. How might your faith community respond to animal welfare or ethical concerns surrounding animals in ways that align with your theology? What are some first steps you can take to engage your community in this conversation?
3. How do you define healing in the context of pet ministry? What role do you think compassion plays in that healing?
4. What spiritual lessons might we learn from animals—like the donkeys described by Marcia McFee—that could enrich our understanding of discipleship or community life?

---

3. For those interested in certification, see organizations like the Compassion Consortium: https://www.compassionconsortium.org/training.

EPILOGUE

What's Next

We began our ministry in 2007 when we started our first therapy dog training class. At the time we had no idea how our lives would be changed and how the lives of others would be transformed in the process. We've now sponsored almost two decades of therapy dog classes and have no plans to stop. Through our training classes, conducted in four different churches, Gayle has met over five hundred handlers who have a common interest in sharing their dog, their time, and their delight in a ministry to help other people.

Gayle has also experienced special moments with her dogs, like visiting a hospice patient. On the last day that she went to see the woman, Gayle found her near death. As frail as she was, she slipped her hand from under the blanket to touch Gayle's dog Allee one more time. This same dog also made special trips to see a resident of the same facility who was paralyzed. When Gayle placed Allee by his pillow, the man smiled, then cried.

We've seen the healing power of therapy dogs at a Blue Christmas service when hurting guests would hold them closely and weep into their fur, releasing their burdens through this intimate connection. Similarly, delivering pet prayer blankets to people with seriously ill pets has created an unforgettable bond with those who were at their most vulnerable. We've said lots of prayers for pets in the animal hospital emergency room. Some have survived and some have not, but all the pet parents have been thankful that someone cared about them.

We've received requests for prayers and pet blankets from people all over the country because they saw that our ministry had comforted someone near to them who lost a beloved pet. We've seen the gratitude in the eyes of people who were able to get low-cost vaccinations or microchipping for their pets through our donations and financial support.

We value all the relationships we have established with the veterinary community who are so generous to share resources with us. Through our pet ministry, we've also come to know deeply committed professionals who are willing to share their expertise with our community. One of our educational webinars was used as a teaching tool for disaster relief workers to better equip them and provide support for stressed pets after a natural disaster or emergency event.

Finally, we've established relationships with people and their pets that would not have occurred without our animal companions. Together, we are a lay person with a passion for pets and an animal-loving pastor—two people in ministry together. What an adventure! What a joy!

The need is there. What will you do to reach out and fill it? What will your pet ministry look like? Who will be on your team? How many lives will you touch?

APPENDIX: RESOURCES FOR PET MINISTRY

Pet Ministry Assessment Form

This is a guide to help make decisions when starting a pet ministry in either your church or your community.

Things to consider for your church or your community:

- What are the demographics of your community?
- What financial resources are available?
- What type of pets are present in your community?
- What are the pet/animal needs in your community?
- Who are potential community partners? Are there any rescue groups, pet stores, or animal advocates, or other similar opportunities in your community?
- Who are potential veterinary partners? Pet Ministry Areas?

Pet Ministry Areas

After answering these questions, think about which components of a pet ministry are most important initially and which ones might you add later. Here is a sample of some pet ministry initiatives:

Care and Support for Pet Parents

- Pet prayer blankets (fleece throws—sewn or purchased)
- Grief support (who will provide? clergy, trained laity, volunteers?)
- Short-term pet fostering list (coordinate efforts with rescue groups)

Therapy Dog Training—Therapy Animal Training

- Availability of therapy dog or therapy animal certifying organization testing and membership requirements for your location

- Availability of a professional dog trainer or knowledgeable dog trainer
- Resources to pay a trainer if necessary
- Facility space for training and liability coverage
- Coordinator to manage the training program (registration forms, establish classes, proof of healthy animals in class, engage an evaluator, and so forth)
- Coordinator for therapy dogs to participate in faith group activities once dogs are certified

Educational Sessions

- Availability of professionals who will speak on relevant topics
- Technical support for presentations either in-person or online

Service Projects

- Determine community pet needs and ways to meet those needs (food, vaccinations, spay/neuter, microchipping, adoption)
- Develop relationships with professional partners in the community to assist with projects
- Designate coordinator for professional, physical and medical resources for projects
- Explore projects to secure resources for emergency veterinary expense fund

Pet Events

- Blessing of the Animals—early October to celebrate the Feast of St. Francis of Assisi
- World Pet Memorial Day—second Tuesday in June

Advocacy

- Animal welfare, including education about animal needs
- Rescue and rehoming
- Animal rights

Pet Ministry Implementation: A Step-By-Step Guide

Get Organized

- Gather a core team to explore ideas for starting a Pet Ministry.
- Pray.
- Complete the Pet Ministry Assessment Form.
- Gather facts and statistics to support your ideas.
- Capture your vision in a document that includes first steps, what you'd like to add, and long-term plans, as well as the impact it will have on people's lives.
- Consider initial and long-term financial expenses and explore resources for funding.
- Review how pet ministry might intersect with other ministries—hospitality, service, congregational care, evangelism, and education.

Make a Presentation

- Visit with potential leadership allies for input as to how a pet ministry might work best in your setting.
- Schedule an initial visit with the senior pastor or leadership staff.
- Make a presentation to the key leadership to share information and get their support.
- Once approval has been obtained to proceed, plan a media campaign for a launch date.

Educate the Congregation and the Community

- Contact the communications department for assistance with preparing educational material, both printed and digital, establishing launch timelines, and utilizing social media and electronic communication tools, both internally and externally. In smaller settings, this might be the office staff or volunteers.
- Anticipate any resistance that people may have, including fear of pets, allergies, harm/liability concerns, and cleanliness.
- Look for creative ways to educate and address those concerns.
- Put together a pet ministry team that is representative of your community (for example, include various age groups, people of different ability levels, and a diverse group of people who have cats, dogs, and other pets). Include members of the congregation as well as people in the community (veterinarians, clinic managers, pet supply business owners, rescue groups, and nonprofits).

Launch

- The pastor may plan a sermon or sermon series around animals for the launch date.
- Provide pet ministry hand-out cards explaining the ministry as well as sign-up sheets available for people who are interested in helping.
- Make sure your team is available on launch date to answer any questions by the community.
- If planning to use therapy dogs, make sure you have signs explaining that the animals are trained, tested, and certified.

Good Manners Around Therapy Dogs

Certified therapy dogs have been tested for obedience, good behavior around people of all ages, good behavior around other dogs, and are comfortable with medical equipment. Their job is to love you and to let you pet them.

Their presence is an opportunity to learn how to care for God's animals and creation and to receive affection too. These are some simple guidelines to remember around therapy dogs.

No Food. Therapy dogs are not allowed to eat a treat when they are working.

Be Gentle. Dogs are not stuffed animals. Don't grab, hug or squeeze too tight.

Ask before you pet. Therapy dogs are to be petted but it's always good to ask first.

Wait your turn. Don't gang up on a therapy dog. Only a few visitors at a time.

Be careful. Don't kiss a dog on the nose or stick your face in theirs.

(This list was inspired by and partially adapted from Jon Katz.)

Resources for Pet Loss

Recommended Books

- *Grieving the Death of a Pet* by Betty J. Carmack
- *Animals in Spirit: Our Faithful Companions' Transition to the Afterlife* by Penelope Smith
- *Coping with Sorrow on the Loss of Your Pet* by Moira Anderson Allen
- *Dog Heaven* by Cynthia Rylant (for children)
- *Cat Heaven* by Cynthia Rylant (for children)
- *Good Grief: On Loving Pets, Here and Hereafter* by E. B. Bartles
- *Going Home: Finding Peace When Pets Die* by Jon Katz
- *Sacred Sendoffs* by Sarah Bowen
- *Goodbye, Friend: Healing Wisdom for Anyone Who Has Ever Lost a Pet* by Gary Kowalski
- *Remember Rafferty* by Joy Johnson (for children)
- *Saying Goodbye to Your Angel Animals: Finding Comfort after Losing Your Pet* by Allen Anderson and Linda Anderson
- *Saying Good-bye to the Pet You Love* by Lorri A. Greene and Jacquelyn Landis
- *The Kingdom of Heart: A Pet Loss Journal* by Patty L. Luckenbach
- *The Loss of a Pet: A Guide to Coping with the Grieving Process When a Pet Dies* by Wallace Sife

Grief Rituals and Remembering Your Pet

It is important to grieve after the loss of an animal who has been such a special member of your family and one with which you had such deep bonds. These are some ways to mourn:

- Designate a sacred space in your home to remember your pet. Include photos, collar/tags, special toys, and so forth.
- Plant a tree or flower in memory of your pet and watch it grow.
- Make a donation to an animal shelter or rescue group in your pet's name.
- Write a letter or poem to your pet expressing your feelings and memories.
- Keep a journal to record your feelings and document your journey.
- Commission a custom painting of your pet.
- Go for a walk along the same path you took with your pet.
- Make a quilt or wall hanging that could include some of your pet's blankets.
- Search for memorial/cremation jewelry to include our pet's ashes in a pendant and necklace.

Remembrance Services

Consider holding a memorial or remembrance service in your pet's favorite outdoor spot, a sacred space or a community gathering place.

Include readings, music, and stories that capture your pet's personality. Allow friends and family to gather and share memories; they may be grieving too. Saying your pet's name out loud and remembering times together helps with healing.

A good book to use when planning a remembrance service is *Animal Rites, Liturgies of Animal Care* by Andrew Linzey.

Helping Other Pets Cope With Loss

Like humans, pets experience a wide array of emotions. The loss of an animal friend can be difficult for other pets in the household, leading to a period of grief and mourning.

Providing your other pets with extra love and attention can help them adjust to the loss. Comfort them as needed, making sure they have a safe space to relax, minimize their time alone, and give your pet time to process the change in their own way and at their own pace. Sticking to a routine and maintaining structure helps makes them feel secure during a time of uncertainty.

Pets mourn in different ways and not all signs are obvious, but these are some common ways pets grieve:

- Depression
- Decreased energy
- Loss of appetite
- Reduced interest in playing
- Hyperactivity in younger pets
- Increased sleep
- Withdrawal from people and other pets
- Inappropriate elimination within the house
- More affectionate and more clingy
- Vocalizing

Pet Loss and Children

Often the loss of a pet is a child's first experience with death. Involve children in the grieving process with activities like drawing a picture of the pet and inviting them to share their favorite memory. Take them for a walk and talk about the pet. Let them know it's ok to be sad.

Be mindful of ways children may react to the loss such as:

- Persistent difficulties with routine activities at home or school

- Preoccupation with thinking about the pet
- Deep, prolonged sadness or depression
- Wondering or questioning about where the pet is, which often includes questions about God

(A good book to share with a child is *Where Does God Live: Questions and Answers for Parents and Children*, particularly Chapter 7, "When My Pet Hamster Elmo Died, Did He Go To Heaven.")

Pet Grief Counseling.

The American Society for the Prevention of Cruelty to Animals (ASPCA) provides a hotline at no charge that connects pet parents with a psychologist to discuss making a decision regarding pet euthanasia and also to help work through pet grief. Call the ASPCA Hotline at 877-474-3310.

Grief Support Websites

The following are a collection of grief support websites for those dealing with the loss of a pet:

- Petloss.com (https://petloss.com/)
- Association for Pet Loss and Bereavement (https://www.aplb.org/)
- Kinship (https://www.kinship.com/)
- Pet Loss Community (https://www.petlosscommunity.com/)
- The Pet Loss Support Page (https://pet-loss.net/)

Writing a Pet Obituary

It is hard to say goodbye to such a treasured member of your family but writing a pet obituary is very healing.

There are no specific rules about writing a pet obituary nor are there time constraints. Even if a pet died several years ago, it is still important to tell your story from the heart.

You might start by jotting down what first comes to mind when you think about your pet. Were they calm and gentle or curious and adventurous? What are some of your memories of how your pet came into your life and what was that first encounter like? What happened to you when you first saw and held your pet? And, how did your life change?

Once you get some initial thoughts on paper, these are other things to consider:

- What was your pet's date of birth or best estimate?
- Are there other surviving family members (human and animal)?
- What were the first days like?
- What was your pet's favorite thing to do? Favorite toys?
- What were your pet's personality characteristics?
- Were there special bonds between your pet and other family member or other animals?
- Did your pet have any special training, awards or certifications?
- End with a loving message to your pet.

Once you have written your pet's obituary, you may want to post it on social media or share it with family and friends as well as others who knew your pet such as your veterinarian, groomer, pet sitter, or pet daycare staff. Be sure to print a copy to place with your pet's mementos as a tangible reminder of their importance in your life.

Sample Remembrance Service for a Pet

For Molly: A Service of Remembrance & Thanksgiving

Officiant: Let us sing to the Lord a new song,

All: A song for all the creatures of the earth.

Officiant: Let us rejoice in the goodness of God,

All: Shown in the beauty of all things.

Officiant: Let us pray.

All: We give thanks, O God, for the gift of Molly's life and for her presence in our lives. Console Kay in her loss, and make our memories of Molly a source of comfort.

Give us courage to entrust her to your tender care, knowing that in every time and season, you use the cycles of life and death, joy and sorrow, beginnings and endings to renew your creation and restore all things to you. Amen.

Reader: A Reading from the Revelation to John.

I saw a new heaven and a new earth: for the first heaven and the first earth were passed away. And he shall wipe away all tears from their eyes; and there shall be no more death, neither sorrow, nor crying, neither shall there be any more pain: for the former things are passed away. And he that sat upon the throne said, Behold I make all things new. I am Alpha and Omega, the beginning and the end.

Officiant: Loving God you created us and placed us on the earth to be stewards of all living things, therefore let us proclaim your glory,

All: O God, how wonderful are the works of your hands.

Officiant: O God, we thank you for the animals that share in your world, that inhabit the skies, the earth and the sea.

All: They share in the fortunes of human existence and play an important part in human life. We remember how animals were saved from the flood and afterwards were a part of the covenant with Noah. We recall a giant fish saved Jonah; ravens brought bread to Elijah; animals were included in the repentance of Nineveh; and animals share in your redemption of all your creation.

Officiant: Blessed are you, O Lord of the Universe; for the sake of our comfort you give us domestic animals as companions, and you give us the ability to train them to help us in our work.

All: Let us be thankful for all therapy dogs, and especially for Molly and Kay's ministry among your people, and for the many lives she and Kay have touched, bringing hope and love to those who need your special healing touch through hands and paws united. In the name of Christ. Amen.

Time for Stories and Thanksgiving

Officiant: Let us pray.

Holy Creator, give us eyes to see and ears to hear how every living thing speaks to us of your love. In wisdom you made all your creatures, in your goodness you have called us to be their stewards.

We are grateful for the blessings Molly brought to our lives and to the lives of so many others.

Give Kay sure confidence and faith, that she may know the consolation of your love.

Even in our sorrow, we have cause for joy, for we know that all that dies on earth shall live again in your new creation.

All: **We commit Molly into your loving hands.**

Officiant: Every living thing is yours and returns to you. Gentle God: fragile is your world, delicate are your creatures, great is your love which bears and redeems us all. Amen.

Animal Chaplains

Animal chaplaincy, begun about thirty years ago, is a growing form of pastoral care that holds presence and space for people to process their emotions surrounding their animal friends. Animal chaplains describe their work as "companioning" rather than "counseling."

These are some animal chaplaincy training programs:

- Association for Veterinary Pastoral Education (https://petchaplain.com/)
- Compassion Consortium (https://www.compassionconsortium.org/)

Another resource for animal chaplains is Sacred Sendoffs (https://www.sacredsendoffs.com/). This website features a memorial ritual kit for animal loss.

Finally, we recommend the work of Rev. Dr. Beth Cooper. She is a specialist in animal and human holistic health, and relief from pain, trauma, and religious abuse. Her approach to healing applies training in disciplines that integrate body, mind, and spirit.

Dr. Cooper is a graduate of Duquesne University, Perkins School of Theology, and Wesley Theological Seminary. She holds a dozen certifications, and credentials in holistic health practices for people and animals. She is available for consultations, appointments, retreats, and other events. She can be reached at (619) 851-5235, or via email at drbacooper@gmail.com Her website is bewellsphere.com.

Emergency Preparedness for Your Pet

Assemble an Emergency Kit for Your Pet (Adapted from the Red Cross)

Keep items in an accessible place and store them in sturdy containers so that they can be carried easily.

Your kit should include:

- Sturdy leashes, harnesses, and/or carriers to transport pets safely and ensure that they can't escape.
- Food, drinking water, bowls, cat litter/pan, and a manual can opener if your pet eats canned food.
- Medications and copies of medical records stored in a waterproof container.
- A first aid kit.
- Current photos of you with your pet(s) in case they get lost. Since many pets look alike, this will help to eliminate mistaken identity and confusion.
- Information on feeding schedules, medical conditions, behavior problems, and the name and number of your veterinarian in case you need to foster or board your pets.
- Pet beds and toys (if easily transportable).

Help Pets Recover After an Emergency

Your pet's behavior may change dramatically after a disaster. They may become aggressive or defensive. Be aware of their well-being and protect them from hazards to ensure the safety of other people and animals. Here are some helpful guidelines:

- Watch your animals closely and keep them under your direct control as fences and gates may have been damaged.
- Pets may become disoriented, particularly if the disaster has affected scent markers that normally allow them to find their home.
- Be aware of hazards at nose and paw or hoof level, particularly debris, spilled chemicals, fertilizers, and other substances that might not seem to be dangerous to humans
- Consult your veterinarian if any behavior problems persist.

National Pet Holidays

January 2	Happy Mew Year for Cats
February	Pet Dental Health Month
February 3	National Golden Retriever Day
March 23	National Puppy Day
April 11	National Pet Day
April 30	National Therapy Animal Day
May	National Dog Mom Day (Second Saturday)
May 20	National Rescue Dog Day
June	World Pet Memorial Day (Second Tuesday)
July	National Lost Pet Prevention Month (July 4 is highest single day for pets to go missing)
July 10	National Kitten Day
August 26	National Dog Day
September 17	National Pet Bird Day
October	National Adopt a Shelter Dog Month
October 29	National Cat Day
November	National Animal Shelter Appreciation Week (First full week)
December 10	National Animal Rights Day
December 27	National Visit the Zoo Day

ACKNOWLEDGMENTS

New Tricks originated from treasured relationships—professional, spiritual, and familial. Thanks to encourager-editor Susan Salley, who recommended us to Upper Room Books; to Michael Stephens, Ben Howard, Dylan White, Deborah Arca, Lisa Lehr, and Eliana Teel—all keepers; and to our friend Cary Smith, who created the book's cover art.

We are grateful to the United Methodist congregations that supported and inspired this book. Special thanks to Adam Hamilton, senior pastor of Resurrection UMC, whose annual leadership event introduced us to collaborative partners Kathy O'Dowd and Linda Haney. We also thank Quapaw Quarter UMC, Trinity UMC, Pulaski Heights UMC, and Pinnacle View UMC. Finally, we are deeply appreciative of Bishop Laura Merrill for her support and enthusiasm about pet ministry, and of the Arkansas Conference communications staff—Amy Ezell, Day Davis, and Danielle Adkisson—for their invaluable help.

Thanks to Yvonne Koehler, who taught our first therapy dog class; Melissa McMath Hatfield, who creates educational pet webinars; and Pam Padgett, our faithful therapy dog evaluator. Thanks also to Brenda Guillet and Holly Pettit for generously donating their time to teach dog training classes; to Kay Russell, whose dog Molly was in the first therapy dog class; and to Stephanie Dungey, a valued community partner.

We also thank Drs. Jon and Jeanie Kendal, who deepened our understanding of animal service; Rev. Martha Taylor, who taught us about the healing gifts of horses; Rev. Dr. Beth Cooper; and our veterinarians—Dr. Cole Bierbaum (Betsy's vet) and Dr. Douglas Winter. (Gayle's vet).

Thanks to my two brothers who, with me, grew up loving our dog Penny, and to my husband, Paul—a wonderful encourager and a great pet parent. Thank you for your patience and always saying "yes!" —Gayle

I love the "litter" I grew up in—four siblings who taught me to love everyone, especially underdogs. Thanks to my spouse, Victor, and our boys—Penn, Wyatt, Sullivan, and Aubrey. —Betsy

ACKNOWLEDGMENTS